The Cultured Landscape

Landscape is integral to, and intertwined with, all aspects of human life. In this book Sheila Harvey and Ken Fieldhouse have brought together a distinguished team of writers and practitioners to explore important philosophical questions about the aims, values and purposes of landscape architecture.

Drawing from a range of unique theoretical and philosophical perspectives, these essays offer fresh insights on current themes to reach a conclusion on how landscape architecture is meeting the challenges of today's cultural conditions. With the freedom to explore new aspects of the subject from a wide base of knowledge, the writers and editors together encourage innovative ways of thinking about quality in landscape design.

A thought-provoking collection from key writers and commentators, this book fuses theory and practice in an original assessment of the philosophy of the landscape. It features authoritative and distinctive contributions from Martha Schwartz, Alan Tate, Simon Swaffield, Merrick Denton-Thompson, John Hopkins, Peter Neal and Catharine Ward Thompson, to encourage progressive thinking and stimulate the development of fresh approaches to the art of landscape design.

Sheila Harvey has been Librarian to the Landscape Institute for over 30 years and is the editor of several books on landscape. In 2003 she was awarded the Ken Fieldhouse Memorial Medal by the Landscape Institute for services in promoting landscape architecture.

Ken Fieldhouse led the Landscape Design Trust for nearly two decades until his death. He was a landscape architect, town planner and editor of *Landscape Design* for 20 years, helping to form it into one of the most influential magazines on landscape architecture in the world.

Also available

Contemporary Landscapes of Contemplation

Edited by Rebecca Krinke

Settings and Stray Paths

Marc Treib

Garden History: Philosophy and Design 2000BC–2000AD

Tom Turner

For further information and to order from our online catalogue
visit our website at www.routledge.com

The Cultured Landscape

Designing the environment
in the 21st century

Edited by Sheila Harvey
and Ken Fieldhouse
with John Hopkins

Routledge
Taylor & Francis Group

LONDON AND NEW YORK

First published 2005
by Routledge,
2 Park Square, Milton Park,
Abingdon, Oxon OX14 4RN

Simultaneously published in the USA and Canada
by Routledge
270 Madison Ave, New York, NY 10016

Routledge is an imprint of the Taylor & Francis Group

Typeset in Univers by Bookcraft Ltd Stroud, Gloucestershire
Printed and bound in Great Britain by TJ International Ltd, Padstow, Cornwall

British Library Cataloguing in Publication Data
A catalogue record for this book is available from the British Library

Library of Congress Cataloging in Publication Data
The cultured landscape: desinging the environment in the 21st century/edited by
Sheila Harvey and Ken Fieldhouse.
     p. cm.
  Includes bibliographical references and index.
  1. Landscape architecture–Philosphy. 2. Landscapre assessment.
  I. Harvey, Sheila, 1938– II. Fieldhouse, Ken.
SB472.C85 2005
712'.01–dc22   2004029203

ISBN 0-419-25030-1 (hb)
ISBN 0-419-25040-9 (pb)

In memory of Ken Fieldhouse (1948–2002) –
colleague, friend, landscape architect, publisher and
great communicator.

Contents

Illustration credits

The authors and the publishers would like to thank the following individuals and institutions for giving permission to reproduce illustrations. We have made every effort to contact copyright holders, but if any errors have been made we would be happy to correct them at a later printing.

Art2Architecture ©, 7.4
Carter, Paul ©, 6.12
Cormier, Claude ©, Plates 7, 8
Cramp, Simon ©, 6.3, 6.4
Denton-Thompson, Merrick ©, 6.1, 6.5, 6.8
Eaton, Marcella ©, 3.2, 3.4, 3.11, 3.15, Plates 4, 5
EDAW ©, 7.4
English Nature ©, Plate 1
Hampshire County Council Countryside Service ©, 6.10
Hopkins, John ©, 2.1, 2.2, 7.5
Humphreys, Susan ©, 6.2
Jones, Martin ©, 2.3, 3.3, 3.5, 3.6, 3.7
LDA Design ©, Plates 27, 28
Martha Schwartz Inc. ©, 4.1, 4.2, 4.3, 4.4, 4.5, Plates 9–23
Neal, Peter ©, 7.1, 7.2, 7.3, 7.4, 7.6, 7.7, Plates 24, 25
Read, Claire ©, 6.11
Smith, Ray ©, 6.6, 6.7, 6.9
Swaffield, Simon ©, 1.1, 1.2, 1.3, 1.4, 1.5
Tanguay, Louise ©, Plate 8
Tate, Alan ©, 3.1, 3.8, 3.9, 3.10, 3.12, 3.13, 3.14, Plates 3, 6
Tate Hopkins Landscape Architects and Planners ©, Plate 2
Toms, Rachel ©, Plate 26
Vézina, J.-F. ©, 3.6, 3.16, Plate 7
Ward Thompson, Catharine ©, 5.1, 5.2, 5.3, 5.4, 5.5, 5.6, 5.7
West 8 ©, Plate 4

Contributors

Merrick Denton-Thompson is the Assistant Director of Environment for Hampshire County Council. He has worked for local government all his professional career. At the council he is responsible for rural affairs, land management, coastal zone management and national parks. He is also responsible for a range of business support services to the Environment Department. He directs the Rural Pathfinder scheme for the South East Region and represents the LGA on the Agri-environment Review Group, advising ministers on the new agri-environment schemes to be launched in the spring of 2005. He is founding Trustee and Chairman of the Executive Committee for the Learning Through Landscapes Trust, Trustee for the Place2Be and Trustee for Marwell Zoo. He was awarded an OBE in 2002 for services to education.

John Hopkins is a partner in LDA Design, a broadly based environmental planning, urban design and landscape architecture practice. He leads its London office. He is a landscape architect, urban designer and environmental planner with expertise in master planning through to site design and implementation. He has practised in Malaysia, Australia, Hong Kong and the United States. He is a graduate of Louisiana State University, a Corporate Member of the American Society of Landscape Architects, a Fellow of the Landscape Institute, a Churchill Fellow in Urban Design and an adviser to CABE Space. He sits on the CABE and South East England Regional Design Review Panels and was a member of the Executive Board of the Urban Design Alliance from 1999 to 2004. He has been a consultant to the Royal Parks Agency since 1993 and is directing the restoration of several historic parks. He directed the preparation of several environmental infrastructure strategies covering the whole of the Thames Gateway, and continues working on significant masterplans in the Gateway and in Edinburgh. His work at Warrington town centre won several national and regional awards from the RTPI and the Civic Trust and the British Council for Shopping Centres' Overall Environment Award. He is external examiner at Manchester Metropolitan University and teaches part-time at The Bartlett, University College, London. He lectures widely at universities and conferences in Europe, the United Kingdom and the United States, writes regularly for the professional press, and has made contributions to several books on urban and landscape design.

Peter Neal is a landscape architect and currently leads a national advisory programme for CABE Space. Initially trained at Manchester University, he completed a master's degree in landscape planning and ecology at Harvard University's Graduate School of Design. He has worked with several design consultancies, including the ROMA Design Group in San Francisco and EDAW in London, and recently completed a book on urban villages while working for The Prince's Foundation.

Martha Schwartz is a landscape architect and artist with a major interest in urban projects and the exploration of new design expression in the landscape. Her background is both in fine arts and in landscape architecture. She has more than 25 years of experience as a landscape architect and artist on a wide variety of projects with a variety of world-renowned architects. She is the recipient of numerous awards and prizes, including a fellowship from the Urban Design Institute, several design awards from the American Society of Landscape Architects, visiting residencies at Radcliffe College and the American Academy in Rome, and a recent Honorary Fellowship from the Royal Institute of British Architects in London. She is also an Adjunct Professor of Landscape Architecture at the Harvard University Graduate School of Design.

Simon Swaffield is Professor of Landscape Architecture and Group Leader of Landscape Architecture at Lincoln University, New Zealand. He is a registered landscape architect and Fellow of the New Zealand Institute of Landscape Architects. He has professional experience in public authorities and housing associations and in environmental consultancy in the United Kingdom, Canada and New Zealand. His research areas include social and cultural dimensions of landscape ecology and land-use change, theory in landscape architecture and urban and regional sustainability.

Alan Tate is Head of the Department of Landscape Architecture at the University of Manitoba and a former President of the Landscape Institute of the United Kingdom. He has degrees in planning and landscape architecture and has spent more than twenty years managing landscape consultancies specializing in urban park planning and design in Hong Kong and London. He is author of *Great City Parks* (Spon Press 2001).

Catharine Ward Thompson was educated at Southampton and Edinburgh Universities. She has practised as a landscape architect in Canada and in the United Kingdom. She was Head of the School of Landscape Architecture at Edinburgh College of Art/Heriot-Watt University for more than a decade and continues to teach in the School and to coordinate its PhD programme as a Research Professor. In this role she directs OPENspace, the research centre for inclusive access to outdoor environments, founded in 2001. She is a Fellow of the Landscape Institute and of the Royal Society for the Encouragement of Arts, Manufactures and Commerce (RSA), a Landscape Adviser to the Forestry Commission and a Trustee of the Landscape Design Trust.

Preface

Several years have elapsed since Ken Fieldhouse and I first started to discuss the format and possible content of this book. Sadly, Ken's untimely death in May 2002 brought the project to a halt. However, after some reflection I decided that the sensible thing would be to go ahead with the book and attempt to get it completed, for the sake of all concerned. Some of the contributors had been with us from the beginning (Simon Swaffield, John Hopkins, Catharine Ward Thompson and Merrick Denton-Thompson) and were happy to aim for completion in spite of the inevitable delays. I was greatly encouraged to recruit Alan Tate, Martha Schwartz and Peter Neal to complete the line-up. Alexander Garvin kindly agreed to write the Foreword.

The contributors are drawn from academia, private practice and the public realm and offer both theoretical and personal approaches to their subjects. I am deeply indebted to them all for their stimulating and informative contributions and have personally learnt much from editing and reading their work.

I should also like to thank Caroline Mallinder, our editor at Taylor and Francis, for her patience, encouragement and faith in the project throughout the process. My main debt of gratitude, however, is to John Hopkins, who so generously stepped in to provide much-needed editorial support after Ken's death and whose backing and advice gave me the strength to finish the task.

Sheila Harvey

Foreword

"A sense of enlarged freedom"

Alexander Garvin

The Cultured Landscape is a unique and important collection of essays. Up to now, most books on landscape have been histories of garden design, stories about important public open spaces, biographies of significant designers, or reviews of city and country landscapes. *The Cultured Landscape* takes us beyond the garden and the park, to consider landscapes around the world within an environmental and cultural context.

The significance of globalization is evident in the first sentence of the first essay in the book, when Simon Swaffield writes of pulling out 'a new shoot of clematis', an invasive foreign plant in his native New Zealand. Alan Tate illustrates his points with examples from the world's largest shopping mall in Edmonton, Canada, the Bibliothéque Nationale in Paris, two parks in New York City, and gardens in the Netherlands and Sweden. For Catharine Ward Thompson even the words 'countryside', 'wilderness' and 'landscape' are constructs whose meaning has been evolving in response to communications and information technology. While these authors clearly recognize the importance of international precedents, they imply that 'genius loci' should be pre-eminent, and that an international style such as 20th-century modernism is inappropriate for the 21st century.

Stewardship of the land can be conceived as conservation. There are few places, however, where the land has not been touched by human hands, some places where human hands have created lovely landscapes, and some places where landscape rises to the level of great art. But how does the world obtain such extraordinary places as the Summer Palace in Beijing or the Villa d'Este in Tivoli? Martha Schwartz concentrates on the situation in the United States; Merrick Denton-Thompson on Britain – in both cases these professionals broaden the role of landscape beyond artifacts. Schwartz questions whether the property owner is truly the client, and wonders about the role of the public in altering the landscape designer's initial artwork. Denton-Thompson writes about methods of managing ordinary landscapes so that they welcome ordinary people. Unlike Schwartz, he sees 'little room for an overt design statement,' arguing instead for continuing reinvestment as a means of sustaining a 'multi-functional countryside'.

Over half a century has passed since Christopher Tunnard wrote that it was society's responsibility to cultivate what he called the 'cultural patrimony', or inheritance from one's ancestors. For Tunnard our patrimony included both man-made landscape treasures such as Angkor Wat, Vaux-le-Vicomte, and Mesa Verde, and natural wonders like Victoria Falls, Yosemite, and the Li River in Guangxi. It is our responsibility to select what is significant from our patrimony, nurture and enhance it, and pass on to future generations an environment that is richer, more fulfilling, and more beautiful.

As John Hopkins makes so evident, our patrimony includes the quality of our air and water, energy consumption, the sustenance of entire ecological systems, and (in addition to the physical, cultural and historical) a *political and philosophical* dimension. This leads him to a discussion of ethics and human rights. In fact, Hopkins would have us consider the environment as a whole, not simply just as the land. Stewardship of the environment (the broader definition that Hopkins argues for) requires action. In the United States there are now 1,400 semi-private land trusts specifically established for this purpose. I would not be surprised to see this approach became popular elsewhere.

Frederick Law Olmsted, America's first and pre-eminent landscape architect, argued that parks should be places that bring together the widest range of people and provide them with 'a sense of enlarged freedom'. He believed in the restorative effects of landscape, in terms of both respiratory and mental health, saying: 'the enjoyment of scenery employs the mind without fatigue and yet exercises it, tranquilizes it and yet enlivens it'. Like Olmsted, Hopkins makes an ethical argument for a landscape that will sustain and nurture human life. Moreover, like Olmsted, he is a democrat arguing for an 'open, participatory, transparent' society. Let us hope that the world adopts his philosophy. Whether it does or does not, this volume provides some excellent recommendations.

Introduction

Sheila Harvey

Whether we know it or not, landscape provides the setting for our lives and there-fore directly or indirectly influences everything that we do. There are very few land-scapes that are still entirely natural, untouched by humankind. Our interference, for good or ill, comes in many forms, whether through cutting down parts of the rain-forest or melting the Arctic ice caps, from global warming to urban planning, changing agricultural field patterns, stabilizing a riverbank or simply designing a garden, and it is essential that we are all collectively and individually aware of this. To quote Al Gore, "Our challenge now, which requires the education of us all and the raising of our collective awareness on a global basis, is to restore and save the earth even as we add still more members to the human family."[1]

The human family has grown and developed in different ways and at a different pace throughout the world, with an inevitable movement towards what are perceived as the civilized or sophisticated, yet ever-increasingly tech-nological values of the western world. This can produce feelings of what Thayer calls 'environmental guilt',[2] of which the outward manifestation is the need to save and protect the environment from further unsustainable destruction. However, this in itself gives rise to moral and ethical questions, as noted by Brian Hackett in the 1970s.[3] Should we, for example, try to prevent technical/scientific progress in underdeveloped countries, denying their peoples access to technology that we have since outlawed as ecologically unsound? Extreme environmentalism has to be carefully balanced against development or prog-ress for short-term economic gain.

As is pointed out in this book, there are many different ways of seeing and experiencing landscape, depending on factors such as personal background, ethnicity, education, and temperament. We are also influenced – some might say brainwashed – by the media in its various manifestations: television, film, books, theatre, music and songs in particular, such as the popular romanticism of those examples associated with Ireland, Scotland, Paris, New York, Vienna and so on. All of the above colour both our conscious and subconscious reactions to place. It may be helpful in this context to consider Geoffrey Jellicoe's frequently expressed belief that our experience of landscape works not only at a conscious level but, more importantly, at a subconscious level too.

All of this can influence what people want or expect from their environment; and in the process of planning or designing changing landscapes, the social element must never be ignored. The element of 'nanny knows best' (whether nanny is the landscape architect or a political authority) should be avoided. Against this, however, is the undeniable fact that those likely to be affected by designed change should have the right to be consulted. It is by now a cliché that the poor are often the last to benefit from any development, but all levels of society must be drawn into the process of consultation if we are to succeed in producing sustainable environments to restore and improve our lives. There are many professionals who could (and do) aid this move to universal awareness, but the landscape architect would seem to be in an especially privileged position. James Corner sees "landscape architecture as humankind's primary vehicle for saving the earth; landscape architects are the stewards of the land and of the earth's natural systems; they work to restore health to ecosystems and to ameliorate the increasing environmental stresses found in our cities and countryside."[4]

The thinking that gave rise to this book lay in the belief that there is often a gulf between landscape theory and practice and a real danger that current issues in society are not being adequately addressed by landscape architects; that this book might help to relate modern cultural and landscape theory to applied landscape design; and to place the application and practice of landscape architecture firmly within the social, philosophical and cultural background from which it derives and hopefully serves. At the very least it might contribute to a healthy debate and indicate positive roles for landscape architects.

The first part of the book addresses cultural, philosophical and moral implications of landscape. Swaffield discusses the complexity of landscape meanings and values, the ways in which we see or experience landscape, our reactions to preservation versus change and the empowerment of communities. The last aspect especially is a recurring theme throughout the book. Hopkins' contribution examines the historical development of ethics and landscape perception; how the landscape architect intervenes and by what right; conflict in acting for the good of self versus others, which is picked up in practical terms in the section on design context; the importance of ecology, community and art as a cohesive whole; and the need for global solutions in which there is a vital and central role for landscape architects. These first two chapters form the theoretical background and may be simply expressed as (1) how we see and relate to our landscape, and (2) intervention by whom, for whom.

Outstanding examples of landscape design do not occur in a vacuum or even by chance. They require encouragement through appreciation of their values and stimulation to demonstrate creative options. This is shown in Part 2, where Tate traces the development of the design context, arguing that the achievement of a "radical approach must be based on a clear under-standing of the place to be changed" and "involves the creation of external places for purposes of utility with beauty". Key values and movements are examined through the work of practitioners, thinkers and critics. As an individual practitioner, Schwartz follows on with a personal view on the relationship between designer, client and end-user. She discusses the interaction required for handling public schemes successfully; the pressure on landscape architects to relate to the agendas of others, and the ethical, economic and aesthetic conflicts that can arise; and the importance of art in landscape design.

Part 3 moves on to the wider environmental agenda and who stands to benefit from the landscape design process. Through a detailed study of land-scape as shaping people's lives and identities and their reactions to landscape, Ward Thompson discusses the use of public space: streets versus parks; rural and urban; the combination of old and new values, including the effect of infor-mation technology on our lives; cultural diversity; and national and international initiatives – "landscape architecture is about process, about change, whether managing the slowly evolving change of biological systems or the rapid change of development intervention". Denton-Thompson then offers a personal view of how landscape design fits into the environmental agenda and whether or not its practitioners are successfully engaging with social issues at both local and national levels. Many of the environmental issues that have become so familiar in recent years are set to grow in magnitude as we address problems of managing finite resources and aspire to an ever-improving quality of life.

In the final chapter Neal and Hopkins draw upon the earlier essays to conclude with an imaginative prediction for the directions that creative land-scape can take in the 21st century.

We are now living in a world where natural and man-made disasters abound, where in spite of (some might say because of) enormous scientific and technical advances, we are constantly beset by war, global warming, hurricanes, floods, nuclear accidents – the list, sadly, is endless. There is an urgent need for us to recognize the importance of our environment in order to sustain any quality of life, indeed life itself. As this book demonstrates, landscape architects have a vital part to play in the prevention, reconstruction and stewardship that will help to prevent further degradation and disaster and have a key role as players in the design, management and science of all things environmental.

Notes

1 Gore, A. *Earth in the balance, forging a new common purpose.* 2nd edn. London, Earthscan Publications, 2000.
2 Thayer, R. L. *Gray world, green heart.* New York, Wiley, 1994.
3 In S. Harvey (ed.), *Reflections on landscape.* Aldershot, Gower Technical Press, 1987.
4 Corner, J. 'Landscape as question', *Landscape Journal*, vol. 11, 2 (Fall), 1992, p. 163.

Part 1

The theoretical, cultural and
philosophical implications
of landscape

Chapter 1

Landscape as a way of knowing the world

Simon Swaffield

Introduction

Turning my back to the cold southerly, I bend down to pull out a new shoot of clematis that is starting to climb into the young ngaio. It seems never ending, this rooting out of the weeds that threaten to overwhelm our attempts at landscape restoration. I reflect upon the patterns of regrowth on the slopes above: the landscape alternates between the rich olive greens of the dry bush surviving in the gullies and a vivid yellow of the gorse and broom spreading into the pasture on the open spurs. Some landscape ecologists argue that these aggressive colonisers can act as useful nurse species for bush regen-eration, but farmers see the loss of productive pasture as a betrayal of their past efforts. Children's voices rise from the creek, where my son and a school friend are playing. They appear through the trees, one Pakeha and the other Maori; the two cultures whose histories have interwoven here for over 200 years. There's an evocative story about a family of early European settlers and their struggle to survive in the strange landscape, helped by the local Maori community. The site of the original cottage is across the creek, and the cottage long gone: visitors often focus upon the old weatherboard house on the neigh-bouring section, but that was brought over from the city on a truck only a few years ago. As I return to the study my attention waivers,

3

Simon Swaffield

and I gaze out of the window. The removal of the old willow has opened up the view of the bay, and we can now see the outline of the crater rim stretching away southwards, a dramatic landscape framed by the remaining trees …

1.1
There are many ways of knowing a landscape. Otoromiro/ Governor's Bay, Aotearoa/New Zealand

Personal narrative is a common opening device for landscape texts. W. G. Hoskins looked out from his study across the English landscape he loved and mourned in his classic historical account *The Making of the English Landscape* (1955). So also did Raymond Williams, in *The Country and the City* (1973), but his interpretation of what he saw was very different. In both cases, the perspective was of the informed observer. In his novels, Williams used a very different narrative form, expressing his intense feelings for the landscape of the Welsh borders through the experiences of a fictional character (1960). Denis Cosgrove (1988) also focused upon the experience of a familiar landscape, opening his account of culture and symbolism in landscape with a more prosaic account of Saturday morning at the local town centre. This grounded approach echoes the evocative accounts of the everyday landscape so typical of the American writer J. B. Jackson in *Discovering the Vernacular Landscape* (1984).

My own opening account has elements both of the detached observer of landscape and of landscapes felt and experienced. There is a hint of

4

the science of landscape as process and pattern, and of landscape design and management interventions; of the social and political relationships that underlie landscape, and of different cultural readings of landscape. These are not only different forms of landscape narrative but also different ways of knowing the world.

For most readers the forms of landscape description in the introductory paragraphs will be familiar. But the environmental setting will be strange. Why is a southerly wind cold? Isn't it normally warm? And why is he complaining about clematis? Isn't that a native plant? The reason becomes clearer as the account continues. For I am writing in a setting that is about as far from the European landscape, geographically, as it is possible to get. My home in New Zealand is on the opposite side of the globe, but the familiarity of form and sentiment reveals how the language of landscape now extends around the world. Some argue that it always has, in different guises (Bender 1993). One result of the translation of landscape thinking into different settings can be a sharpening of points of difference (Seddon 1997), and a central theme of this chapter is the tension between landscape as conventional and typically privileged knowledge and other expressions of landscape as a way of knowing the world. First, however, it is necessary to briefly address the idea of landscape.

Landscape is a familiar term that is rich and evocative, but also complex and at times confusing. It is both "an old and pleasant word in common speech" and "a technical term in special professions" (Meinig 1979: 33). In his much quoted article, the geographer Donald Meinig identified ten different ways of thinking about landscape and its meaning (discussed in more detail in Chapter 2). He opens his review by noting that "landscape is composed not only of what lies before our eyes but what lies within our heads' (1979: 34) and in this captures something of the problem facing policy makers, scholars, designers, and students of landscape. "Landscape is not merely the world as we see it, it is a construction, a composition of that world. Landscape is a way of seeing the world" (Cosgrove 1984: 13). Herein, however, lies its greatest potential. Landscape, argues James Corner, is "both spatial milieu and cultural image … a medium that is embedded and evoked within the imaginative and material practices of different societies at different times" (1999: 5).

The nature of landscape has been variously interpreted. Its etymological development from the origins of the word in Indo-European languages to its contemporary meanings has been well documented (Jackson 1984; Stilgoe 1982; Relph 1981; Corner 1999; Olwig 2002). The shifts in meaning that took place in the 16th and 17th centuries are particularly significant, as 'landscape' was translated from German through Dutch into English. Central to this is the evolution from *Landschaft*, expressing experiential and organisational relationships between people and land, to *landschap/landskip*, which relates to the more abstract and pictorial representation of land. Kenneth Olwig (2002) demonstrates how these shifts of meaning were intensely political and were linked to the emergence of the nation state. Contemporary usage of 'landscape' now carries with it traces of active, experiential, and detached, pictorial meanings, although the emphasis varies with the context.

One common theme in much contemporary writing, however, is that landscape provides a useful way, or ways, of knowing the world (Seddon 1997). It gives us a framework of understanding within which to describe and analyse what we see of, and feel about, the environment in which we live (Swaffield 2002). Landscape also provides a systematic basis for understanding the spatial patterns and processes we see around us, and the way that people adapt the environment to their needs and desires. Understanding landscape therefore complements and provides an important counterpoint to other ways of knowing.

The aim of this chapter is to review some different ways in which landscape embodies knowledge. It offers two contrasting evaluations of the significance of landscape as a way of knowing. On the one hand, landscape understanding can be seen as an integral part of modern science, culture and society. As such it has the advantage of being familiar, largely unquestioned, and linked to other forms of conventional knowledge about the environment. On the other hand, landscape knowledge can be used as the basis for a critique of aspects of modern life. It may challenge taken-for-granted assumptions about what is valued, and can provide a voice for people whose concerns may not otherwise be heard. The striking feature of landscape as a way of knowing the world is that it fulfils both these conventional and radical roles.

There is, however, a price to be paid for such multivalence. A number of scholars highlight the tensions *within* landscape, between a role they describe as "an elitist (and illusory) 'way of seeing'" and its expression of "a vernacular (and realistic) 'way of life'" (Daniels 1987: 329). Although some argue that, as a consequence, landscape is an unhelpful concept, there is growing realisation that this ambiguity, even duplicity (Daniels 1987), in landscape is itself a reflection of the more general complexity of culture. Hence the ability of landscape to generate powerful feelings of belonging, of aesthetic pleasure, and of wonder at the complexity of ecology, while also expressing the relations within and between societies, is perhaps its greatest strength. The essential qualifier to this claim is that the relationships must be critically scrutinised and acknowledged.

To accept the ambiguity and severally layered meanings of landscape does not excuse us from careful examination of them and their origins. Rather, it obliges us to pay rather greater attention to them than we have done in the past, for it is in the origins of landscape as a way of seeing the world that we discover its links to broader historical structures and processes and are able to locate landscape study within a progressive debate about society and culture.

(Cosgrove 1984: 15)

Thinking about and through landscape can be a painful as well as pleasurable experience.

A second consequence of the multivalence in the concept of landscape is the way it is continually evolving in its meanings and interpretations. The tensions between the different sides of landscape are dynamic. Michel Conan (1997) notes that landscape painting was reported to have reached the end of its role in the avant-garde of culture in the 1970s, yet only a decade later landscape is experiencing a renaissance as a form of art and culture:

> This supposed death and rebirth of landscape painting is yet another twist in the long history of landscape ideas … It shows how landscape ideas reflect changing ideas about nature, causality, urban life, relations between social classes, and between men and gods. This may warn us against any simple attribution of meaning to landscape as if it were a thing or fact.

(Conan 1997: 165)

James Corner argues that it is precisely the ideas *within* landscape that give it the potential to be an active agent of culture:

> Landscape reshapes the world not only because of its physical and experiential characteristics but also because of its eidetic content, its capacity to contain and express ideas and so engage the mind. Moreover, because of its bigness – in both scale and scope – landscape serves as a metaphor for inclusive multiplicity and pluralism, as in a kind of synthetic 'overview' that enables differences to play out. In these terms, landscape may still embrace naturalistic and phenomenological experience but its full efficacy is extended to that of a synthetic and strategic art form …

(Corner 1999: 1–2)

Landscape is therefore a multivalent form of knowledge. It does not sit easily within any single discipline, nor does it offer only one perspective upon the world. This plurality creates tension, as the knowledge within landscape and the imperatives for action that it brings can lead to diverse outcomes. It is thus contested ground. Nonetheless, as I hope to illustrate below, the knowledge about the world embedded in different conceptions of landscape is rich and wide ranging.

Landscape as a way of knowing

There have been several classifications of landscape as a way of knowing. Tom Turner (1982–3) identified three categories: the artists' landscape (scenery), the geographers' landscape (a tract of land) and the designers' landscape (a planned park or garden). Edward Relph (1981) identified six meanings of landscape, also linked to different disciplines (landscape as object, features in an area, record of history, townscape, meaning of environment, and ideology of ownership). Meinig (1979) extended the role to ten "versions of the same scene". In tracing the evolution of contemporary meanings of landscape in New Zealand, Swaffield and O'Connor (1986) distinguished between landscapes conceived (i.e. mental conceptions of land), landscapes perceived (i.e. phenomena defined by eye) and 'holistic' landscape (i.e. integrated understanding). This classification is adapted and extended below, in the recognition that landscape knowledge can be grounded in different dimensions of human existence: mind, eye, imagination, body and hand (action). These dimensions are not mutually exclusive but provide a framework for different ways of knowing landscape.

Land(scapes) of the mind

One of the most conventional ways of knowing through landscape is as a synthesis of conceptual knowledge about land. An account of 'landscape' describes how we understand the character of an area of land, in a biophysical sense: its form, how it functions, and what this can tell us as a record of past natural and human activity. It is knowledge of the world that is systematically recorded, mapped, measured, abstracted and classified.

For geomorphologists and earth scientists, landscape is a way of understanding the complex interrelationships between soils and landforms (Soons and Selby 1982). The 'landscape' approach to land evaluation (Mabbutt 1968) is based upon identifying distinctive attributes and qualities within an area or region, and the search for distinctive character has also extended into analysis of the overall features of a region, both 'natural' and 'cultural' (Plate 1). Hence regional geographers describe different types of landscape according to the combinations of landform and water, vegetation, towns, cities and other human infrastructure.

The American geographer Carl Sauer (1967) was a particular advocate of the value of landscape as a source for understanding the way different cultures use and change land. "The cultural landscape is fashioned from a natural landscape by a cultural group. Culture is the agent, the natural area the medium, the cultural landscape the result" (cited in Roberts 1994: 133). In this way of knowing, landscape provides a form of 'text' that can be read by the discerning expert and that contains within it an extensive record of past human activity and intent. "The English landscape itself, to those who know how to read it aright", wrote the landscape historian W G Hoskins, "is the richest historical record we possess" (1955: 14).

The development of systems thinking during the past 30–40 years has also informed landscape understanding, and the conceptualisation of landscape as an environmental system is central to the emerging discipline of landscape ecology (McHarg 1969; Naveh and Lieberman 1984; Forman and Godron 1986; Thompson and Steiner 1997). Landscape ecology is concerned with the way ecological processes are expressed in landscape patterns over space and time (Forman 1995). Landscape managers increasingly use knowledge derived from landscape ecology in guiding the optimum location and shape of revegetation projects (Hobbs and Norton 1996). Urban ecology is another application where landscape ecological understanding is widely used at a range

1.2
Landscapes of
the eye: Lake
Matheson Scenic
Reserve, Westland,
New Zealand

of scales, from choosing and locating species for land reclamation (Bradshaw et al 1986) to developing city-wide green space plans (Hough 1984).

(Land)scapes of the eye

The idea that landscape is what we *see* constitutes a second way of knowing about the world through landscape. There are several variations. Popular meanings of landscape include a picture of land, a view from a particular point, or as scenery, and the picturesque qualities of land (Chambers 1993; Oxford English Dictionary 1978). This way of knowing emphasises visual perception and includes a concern for landscape aesthetics – that is, what we like about particular landscapes, and why.

The history and critique of landscape as a picture or scenery constitutes a major body of knowledge, incorporating historical and sociological studies of landscape painting, poetry, estate improvement, countryside planning, and tourism and recreation (Hussey 1927; Clark 1949; Barrell 1980; Crandell 1993; Marsden et al 1993; Cosgrove 1984; Conan 1997). In many ways, the 'scenic' approach to landscape constitutes its core meaning in contemporary usage, particularly in Britain. A number of scholars have traced the way the idea of landscape scenery developed and how painterly terms and concepts were subsequently transferred into estate improvement (Relph 1981; Cosgrove 1984, 1985; Hunt 1992; Olwig 2002).

A second critical extension was from estate improvement into the broader landscape as, according to Horace Walpole, William Kent "leapt the garden fence" and saw all of nature as a garden. The subsequent convergence of the idea of nature with scenic landscape has been extensively documented (Crandell 1993). In particular, the application of 'landscape' sensibility to nature led to a dramatic re-evaluation of 'wild' nature during the 19th century, and to the emergence of a romantic and aesthetic approach to wilderness which underpins much tourism, conservation and recreation to this day (Urry 1990). Similarly, the interpretation and appreciation of rural landscape as scenic countryside, and the implications of agricultural change and urban expansion, have been a focus of landscape studies throughout the 20th century (Marsden et al 1993). The aesthetic principles of estate improvement were also extended into urban parks and gardens in the 19th century and thence into other urban settings (Chadwick 1966; Relph 1981).

The geographer Jay Appleton forged a link between the aesthetic judgement of landscape as scenery and the science of perception. In his classic text *The Experience of Landscape*, he opened with the question "What is it that we like about landscape, and why do we like it?" (1975: 1). Over the subsequent 25 years, much has been learnt empirically about landscape preference, but the question of why remains problematic (Carlson 1993). Appleton proposed a connection between landscape preference and evolutionary survival – to be able to see without being seen – and there has been extensive empirical investigation and theoretical debate over the extent to which 'nature' or 'nurture' shapes landscape preferences (Kaplan and Kaplan 1982, 1989). For many commentators the answer is both (Bourassa 1991), and this raises the question of the social shaping of landscape knowledge.

Landscapes of the imagination

In contrast to the interpretation of landscape as the visual environment seen by all people, some theorists argue that landscape is a socially specific, and frequently privileged, point of view. Hence the idea of landscape as a form of knowledge can only be understood within its social and historical context, and in turn the nature of that knowledge informs us about the relationships between people and between people and land, at that time. "Landscape", argues Cosgrove, "is an ideological concept. It represents a way in which certain classes of people have signified themselves and their world through their imagined relationship with nature, and through which they have underlined and communicated their own social role and that of others with respect to nature" (1984: 15).

For example, some critics argue that many of the classic landscape images of pastoral countryside perpetuate a myth of rural contentment, hiding the

1.3
Landscapes of the
imagination: the
ideological
landscape of Stowe,
Buckinghamshire

patterns of ownership and economic activity that sustain it. The values portrayed, they suggest, are not shared by many less privileged urban and rural people. "A working country is hardly ever a landscape," claimed Williams. "The very idea of landscape implies separation and control" (1973: 120–1). Furthermore, such "Landscapes can be deceptive. Sometimes a landscape seems to be less a setting for the life of its inhabitants than a curtain behind which their struggles, achievements and accidents take place" (Berger and Mohr, cited in Daniels 1987: 335).

The idea that landscape is an imagined relationship or set of relationships between people, land and nature (Gregory 1993) highlights the symbolic dimension of landscape knowledge (Daniels and Cosgrove 1988), and in recent decades there has been increasing interest in the way landscape is represented in particular ways in order to express particular values (Corner 1992). Thus landscape is not a neutral code or body of knowledge that can be read objectively and dispassionately, but rather needs active interpretation (Howett 1987; Daniels and Cosgrove 1988; Duncan and Duncan 1988). 'Imagined' landscapes tell us more about the people whose ideas and values are being projected than they do about land or the processes of perception (Seddon 1997).

Landscapes of the body

Landscapes of the mind emphasise mental abstraction, landscapes of the eye focus upon perception, while landscapes of imagination emphasise the way socially imagined landscapes shape our understanding. Some scholars argue instead that landscape is primarily a way of knowing the world through

1.4
Landscapes of the body: Christianshavn 'free' community, Copenhagen

grounded, everyday experience. Jackson, for example, has highlighted the cultural values and knowledge about the world expressed within the vernacular landscape of America (1984). Others have studied the way people inhabit and experience everyday city, suburban or rural landscapes (Tuan 1977; Whyte 1980; Jacobs 1961).

Jackson's interest was in the essentially utilitarian vernacular land-scapes of America, a focus shared by John Stilgoe, with his exploration of the 'common' landscape (1982). Jane Brown similarly has described the 'everyday' landscapes of Britain (1982). What they all share is a belief that vernacular land-scape can embody 'people's knowledge' of the world. This type of knowledge is being sought and celebrated in many countries to try and resist the globalisation of economy and technology and the bland, corporate, homogen-ised environments it creates (Relph 1976, 1987). In contrast to the privileged view, vernacular landscape is an expression of local identity, familiar places and community (Seamon 1993).

Jackson's work emphasises that the everyday knowledge of the world embedded in vernacular landscape is grounded in human life, not objects (1979), that landscape is, as Cosgrove put it (1984: 35), "not something to look at but to live in, and to live in socially". Discussing the closely related concept of sense of place, for example, Jackson argued:

> I'm inclined to believe that the average American still associates a sense of place not so much with architecture or a monument or a designed space as with some event, some daily or weekly or seasonal occurrence which we look forward to or remember and which we share with others, and as a result the event becomes more significant than the place itself. Moreover I believe that this has always been the common or vernacular way of recognizing the unique quality of the community we live in … It is our sense of time, our sense of ritual, which in the long run create our sense of place, of community.
>
> (Jackson 1994: 159–60)

To which an increasing number of scholars would add our sense of landscape.

"Features and patterns in the landscape make sense to us because we share a history with them" (Lowenthal 1985), and Barbara Bender (1993) documents a range of case studies from around the world which show how local communities 'know' their world through an intimate knowledge of experi-enced landscapes. Anne Whiston Spirn (1998) argues that this grounded land-scape knowledge preceded formal language, and many accounts of indigenous people's everyday lives show how knowledge is integrated through all the senses, 'embodied' rather than conceived or perceived (Bender 1993).

Landscapes of the hand

Jackson drew in particular upon the etymology of *Landschaft* in his conception of landscape as "a composition of man made spaces on the land" (1984).
He focused upon landscapes made through the everyday activities of people
living in communities, described as "shaped land" by Stilgoe (1982); and
the activity of shaping land constitutes a further category of landscape
knowledge.

Olwig (2002) argues that the origin of landscape as *Landschaft* is
fundamentally about customary social practice – the habitation of a place – and
he sees the subsequent tensions within landscape meaning and use as a
tension between the landscape of custom, on the one hand, and attempts to
codify landscape as a more abstract overview of laws and relationships, on the
other. From this perspective, landscapes of the 'hand' express the way knowledge is embedded within everyday social practice, shaping places through the
repeated application of tacit knowledge.

Gardening is a good example of the way accumulated knowledge and understanding of the emotional and experiential qualities of
plants and outdoor spaces has been carried forward through everyday

1.5
Landscapes of the
hand: street
reconstruction,
Berlin, 2001

14

practices. Classic texts by Sylvia Crowe (1981) and others consolidate and interpret this aggregated knowledge of gardens and gardening over many centuries, which in turn expresses enduring human values. Crowe suggests, "Throughout all variations, due to climate, country, history and the natural idiosyncrasy of man, which have appeared in the evolution of the garden through successive civilisations, certain principles remain constant however much their application may change" (1981: 76). Although these principles have become codified through books, they are based upon repeated everyday practice.

Landscapes of the hand are not only expressions of practical convention. They can also be the site of experimentation and exploration. During the 1940s and 1950s and again during the 1980s and 1990s, the garden has been an important vehicle for theoretical debate and challenge. In 1939, Christopher Tunnard argued for a new approach to garden design that matched the modernist revolution that was sweeping through architecture. His call was answered by Thomas Church, Garrett Eckbo, James Rose and Dan Kiley, among others, as they created gardens that expressed the new asymmetrical geometry and free forms of modern art (Treib 1993). The garden has re-emerged again as a site of practical and theoretical experimentation since the 1980s, as artists and poets have rediscovered their potential to provide insight into the broader human condition. Bernard Lassus, for example, has used real and imagined gardens as the base from which to project new poetic possibilities of the relationship between nature and culture (1998), and Spirn has argued for the re-inhabitation of the city as a 'Granite Garden' (1984).

This link between gardens as a form of knowledge grounded in practice and the avant-garde exploration of the landscape idea highlights how different ways of knowing intersect and interweave in landscape. Some authors argue that particular ways of knowing are fundamental and structure the other forms of knowledge. Cosgrove (1984), for example, argued that there is an unavoidable and deep-seated social and historical link between landscape as a 'pictorial' way of knowing the world and the way it is used in geography as an 'objective' description of the character of land, such that what I have called landscapes of the mind carry forward within them an implicit imagined, pictorial landscape. There are also clearly reciprocal links between embodied and shaped landscape. However, the advantage of unfolding the different dimensions of landscape knowledge in this way is that it sharpens our awareness of subtle nuances and variations in the way landscape is known. This becomes particularly important when that knowledge is adopted as the basis for professional activity, in the form of landscape architecture.

Landscape architecture

Landscape architecture is a professional expression of landscape under-standing. It draws on all the forms of landscape knowledge outlined above, with the particular emphasis depending upon individual landscape architects, their background and education, and the situation in which they are practising (Thompson 1999). The knowledge may be used at a range of scales, from a garden to a regional plan. What is common, however, is a commitment to use landscape understanding to change the world in some way, through planning and policy, design, or management. Important new knowledge emerges through this application process. Indeed, design is as valid a way of knowing the world as scientific description or literary criticism (Armstrong 1999), and there are aspects of knowing the world that can only be expressed through design.

In 1950 the American landscape architect Garrett Eckbo set out an agenda for the profession in America that dominated the second half of the 20th century. "Landscapes", he argued, "can only be experienced specifically and directly" (1950: 1). To understand landscape, and to apply that under-standing, landscape architecture needed to recognise and incorporate the scientific method, by which "nothing is ultimately unknowable" (1950: 2). The knowledge that Eckbo sought was practical and functional, as well as aesthetic, and incorporated a strong commitment to enhanced social justice. Landscape knowledge and action were to be the way to a better world, a "Landscape for Living". These ambitions perhaps seem naive today in regard to the role of science, yet Eckbo's life and works show him to be both a visionary and prag-matist (Treib 1993). His essential point was that the act of design provides a convergence of ideas and values within the biophysical and cultural landscape, a belief and focus that continue to be shared by the profession today (Thompson 1999).

In the UK, authors such as Brenda Colvin (1970), Brian Hackett (1971), Nan Fairbrother (1970, 1974) and Geoffrey and Susan Jellicoe (1987) were persuasive advocates for the application of landscape understanding to create a better living environment in the era after the Second World War. In her polemic text *New Lives, New Landscapes* (1970) Fairbrother presented a broad vision of landscape as habitat changed by man. Arguing that the old "much loved" agricultural landscapes celebrated and mourned by Hoskins were outdated remnants of a past agrarian society, Fairbrother called for widespread state intervention to remodel the landscape of Britain for a new industrial society. "Preservation … is seldom a workable policy," she argued (1970: 5). "The new landscapes for our new lives must now be consciously achieved by positive and clear sighted adaption of the habitat to our new industrial condi-tion" (1970: 6).

Some 30 years later, Corner has advocated an equally broad but more critically reflective vision for landscape transformation through design. In *Recovering Landscape* (1999) he argues for the recognition and use of land-scape as a strategic instrument of cultural change. Corner identifies several ways in which this can occur: using landscape design as a form of resistance to the global homogenisation of the environment through the recovery of the specificity of site; using landscape as a focus for environmental debate; using landscape as a medium to develop innovative responses to the effects of de-industrialisation; and using landscape thinking as a way of shaping the infra-structure of the modern megalopolis. The strategic cultural role for landscape that he and others (Turner 1996; Strang 1998) advocate resonates strongly with the earlier visions of Fairbrother and Jellicoe.

Whose knowledge and for what purpose?

Recognising that what we know about landscape relates to why we need to know raises the fundamental question, whose way of knowing does it repre-sent? If landscape is conceived in a broad sense – as the way people experi-ence and make sense of the cultural and biophysical environment – then landscape knowledge is and has been shared by all. Spirn put it like this:

> The language of landscape is our native language. Landscape was the original dwelling: humans evolved among plants and animals, under the sky, upon the earth, near water. Everyone carries that legacy in body and mind. Humans touched, saw, heard, smelled, tasted, lived in, and shaped landscapes before the species had words to describe what it did. Landscapes were the first human texts, read before the invention of other signs and symbols.
>
> (Spirn 1998: 15)

Scholars of more recent vernacular landscapes make a similar point: the setting in which people live and work, whether it be rural, suburban or urban, is a frequently taken-for-granted expression of knowledge upon which our everyday lives are based (Bender 1993).

However, such landscape knowledge is not the same everywhere or over time: each culture, region or community has a distinctive vocabulary of landscape elements and patterns, some of which are widely shared, while others, as we can find to our surprise when we travel, are very specific. Hence although we all possess tacit landscape knowledge, what we know depends upon where and how we live.

So much depends, however, on that modest word 'we'. Spirn and Jackson both focus upon an inclusive idea of landscape, and it is perhaps no coincidence that they are writing in America, where the idea of a popular, somehow democratic landscape is a fundamental part of the national identity. In contrast, one of the dominant features of landscape scholarship in Britain over the past couple of decades has been a sustained critique of the way landscape has evolved as an elitist ideal. Authors such as Williams (1973), Berger (1972), Cosgrove (1984) and Daniels (1987, 1991) have argued that landscape knowledge was originally created by and used for the benefit of the bourgeois classes of Europe during the expansion of capitalism in the 17th and 18th centuries. The translation of aesthetic conventions of landscape painting into estate improvement, and the consequential widespread displacement of rural communities to create the space needed for the expansive parks, has been described by John Barrell as the "dark side" of landscape (1980).

Recognition that landscape and the benefits that flow from it may be socially specific has informed a critique of many other types and subsequent phases of landscape knowledge. Increasing critical attention has been given to the way the idea of landscape has been used as part of European colonisation and imperial expansion around the world (Smith 1960, 1992; Seddon 1994). Landscape conventions have also been implicated in nationalist movements, as particular ways of representing landscape are used to express ideals of nationhood and identity (Matless 1998). Some authors conclude that the links between landscape, nationalism and imperialism constitute a fundamental and fatal flaw in the concept (Mitchell 1994).

Recognition of the class and power relations implicit and explicit in landscape knowledge has also opened up critique of gender relations in landscape (Meyer 1994). The visual emphasis of landscape in particular has been implicated in the more general characterisation of nature as feminine (Rose 1993). From this perspective, landscape as a supposedly objective way of seeing becomes "fundamentally one of patrician control" (Daniels 1987: 330).

The specific links between landscape conventions, estate improvement, surveying techniques and class have also been reframed as part of a critique of modern scientific knowledge. Characterised as a partial, selective and detached way of seeing and representing the world, landscape has become regarded by some critics as an expression of much that is wrong with the modern world. Some authors emphasise the way landscape techniques have been deployed to achieve particular social and political ends (Cosgrove 1985). Others have focused more upon the alienation that arises from such detached forms of knowledge (Relph 1981), arguing that it leads to environments that are hostile and lacking in humanity. In each case, however, the suggestion is that instrumental forms of landscape knowledge are socially and culturally problematic.

The breadth and depth of the materialist critique of landscape as an idea that has emerged from particular social circumstances and still carries with it traces of its origins is compelling in many respects, and yet so also are the arguments for a more constructive, contemporary role for landscape knowledge. Landscape continues to be used as a rallying cry for social and environmental reform, against many of the excesses of modern life. In the 19th century, the translation of landscape conventions into urban parks was linked with a strong philanthropic desire to improve the living conditions of the rapidly growing urban populations (Chadwick 1966). The work of the American landscape architect Frederick Law Olmsted in particular is notable for its vision of a collective public good (Rybczynski 1999).

In more recent decades, social and ecological issues have again stimulated a range of more radical 'landscape' initiatives, in which the science of landscape ecology combines with a focus upon the experiential, everyday landscape of local communities to resist the worse excesses of globalisation (Thompson 1999). An early expression of this reformulation of landscape as a radical challenge to conventional practice was the ecological design approach pioneered in Holland (Ruff 1979) and introduced into the British New Towns in the 1970s (Laurie 1979). Initially, emphasis was placed upon restoration and recreation of largely indigenous woodlands, grasslands and wetlands within the new urban areas, frequently on former industrial or mining sites, with the aim that they would make natural environments more accessible to children and communities (Ruff and Tregay 1982).

Over time, emphasis has shifted to community participation in the re-making of urban landscapes, through organisations such as Groundwork and Common Ground. These initiatives are tangible expressions of a phenomenological commitment to 'dwelling' through landscape, combined with the instrumental knowledge of ecology. Drawing upon both public and private funding, these new vehicles for landscape knowledge contrast dramatically with the 'elitist' history portrayed above, as a fundamental part of their operation is the empowerment of local communities, frequently in lower socioeconomic areas, to become engaged in their local landscape setting.

Bender claims that the experience of landscape is "too important and too interesting to be confined to a particular time, place and class" (1993: 1). While acknowledging its genesis in a particular historical context, and the implications this has had for the way that the concept has been deployed within Europe, she argues that there were even at the same time and place "other ways of understanding and relating to the land – other landscapes" (1993: 2). She continues: "The way in which people – anywhere, everywhere –

understand and engage with their worlds will depend upon the specific time and place and historical conditions. It will depend upon their gender, age, class, caste, and on their social and economic situation. People's landscapes will operate on very different spatial scales … on very different temporal scales." Furthermore, "Each individual holds many landscapes in tension … Landscapes are thus polysemic, and not so much artefact as in process of construction and reconstruction" (1993: 2–3).

Conclusion

Landscape knowledge is therefore both conventional and radical, universal and particular, global and local. In some contexts it sits comfortably within the main-stream of western culture, albeit somewhat on the fringes of the intellectual, industrial and political centres of power. Yet its relationship with the more domi-nant disciplines, professions and interests has always been uneasy, perhaps due to its radical potential. Although landscape can be used to reinforce and extend conventional technical ways of knowing the world, it can also challenge the direction and presumptions of modern technology and economy.

Understanding the phenomenology of everyday landscape, its participatory role within planning and design, and the potential for critique of conventional planning all provide ways to present alternative possibilities about the way we manage and relate to the environment. Landscape can be a way to empower a wider range of participants in the planning and design arena.

At a broader scale, the creative use of landscape representation to project alternative futures for urban form, infrastructure investment, ecological restoration and environmental management can be a powerful counter to the technocratic dominance of other forms of knowledge. The understanding of the particularity and distinction of different local and regional landscapes can provide a point of resistance to the homogenising effects of globalisation (Frampton 1983).

Landscape knowledge is therefore both privileged and grounded. The personal account in the introductory section of this chapter contains within it many different strands and tensions and highlights that it is the interweaving of different understandings within landscape that gives it such cultural potential. In the following chapters, other landscape scholars and professionals share their insights into landscape as a polysemic way of knowing, expanding upon the diversity of landscape within culture and design, illustrating the richness and vitality of its continuing evolution.

Bibliography

Appleton, J. (1975) *The Experience of Landscape*, Old Woking, Surrey: Unwin Brothers.

Armstrong, H. (1999) 'Design studios as research: an emerging paradigm for landscape architecture', *Landscape Review* 5, 2: 5–25.

Barrell, J. (1980) *The Dark Side of the Landscape: the rural poor in English painting 1730–1840*, Cambridge: Cambridge University Press.

Bender, B. (ed.) (1993) *Landscape: Politics and Perspectives*, Oxford: Berg.

Berger, J. (1972) *Ways of Seeing*, Harmondsworth: Penguin.

Bourassa, S. (1991) *The Aesthetics of Landscape*, London: Belhaven Press.

Bradshaw, A.D., Goode, D.A., Thorp, E.H.P. (1986) *Ecology and Design in Landscape*, Oxford: Blackwell.

Brown, J. (1982) *The Everyday Landscape*, London: Wildwood House.

Carlson, A. (1993) 'On the theoretical vacuum in landscape assessment', *Landscape Journal* 14: 51–6.

Chadwick, G.F. (1966) *The Park and the Town: public landscape in the 19th and 20th century*, London: Architectural Press.

The Chambers Dictionary (1993) Edinburgh: Chambers Harrap.

Clark, K. (1949) *Landscape into Art*, Oxford: Oxford University Press.

Colvin, B. (1970) *Land and Landscape*, London: John Murray.

Conan, M. (1997) 'Poetry into landscape: evolving views of the pastoral in painting and poetry from antiquity to the nineteenth century', *Journal of Garden History* 17, 3: 165–70.

Corner, J. (1992) 'Representation and landscape: drawing and making in the landscape medium', *Word & Image* 8, 3: 243–75.

Corner, J. (1999) 'Recovering landscape as critical cultural practice', in J. Corner (ed.) *Recovering Landscape: essays in contemporary landscape architecture*, New York: Princeton Architectural Press.

Cosgrove, D. (1984) *Social Formation and Symbolic Landscape*, London: Croom Helm.

Cosgrove, D. (1985) 'Prospect, perspective and the evolution of the landscape idea', *Transactions of the Institute of British Geographers* 10: 45–62.

Cosgrove, D. (1988) 'Geography is everywhere: culture and symbolism in human landscapes', in D. Gregory and R. Walford (eds), *Horizons in Human Geography*, Totowa, NJ: Barnes and Noble Books.

Crandell, G. (1993) *Nature Pictorialised*, Baltimore: Johns Hopkins University Press.

Crowe, S. (1956) *Tomorrows Landscape*, London: Architectural Press.

Crowe, S. (1981) *Garden Design*, Chichester: Packard.

Daniels, S. (1987) 'Marxism, culture and the duplicity of landscape', in R. Peet and N. Thrift (eds), *New Models in Geography*, vol. II, London: Unwin Hyman.

Daniels, S. (1991) 'The making of Constable country 1880–1940', *Landscape Research* 16, 2: 9–17.

Daniels, S., Cosgrove, D. (1988) *The Iconography of Landscape*, Cambridge: Cambridge University Press.

Duncan, J., Duncan, N. (1988) 'Re(reading) the landscape', *Environment and Planning D* 6: 117–26.

Eckbo, G. (1950) *Landscape for Living*, New York: Dodge.

Fairbrother, N. (1970) *New Lives, New Landscapes*, London: Architectural Press.

Fairbrother, N. (1974) *The Nature of Landscape Design*, Sussex: R. J. Ackford.

Forman, R.T.T. (1995) *Land Mosaics: the ecology of landscapes and regions*, Cambridge and New York: Cambridge University Press.

Forman, R.T.T., Godron, M. (1986) *Landscape Ecology*, New York: Wiley.

Frampton, K. (1983) 'Six points towards an architecture of resistance', in H. Foster, *The Anti-Aesthetic*, Washington, DC: Bay Press.

Gregory, D. (1993) *Geographical Imaginations*, Oxford: Blackwell.

Hackett, B. (1971) *Landscape Planning: an introduction to theory and practice*, Newcastle upon Tyne: Oriel Press.

Hobbs, R., Norton, D.A. (1996) 'Towards a conceptual framework for restoration ecology', *Restoration Ecology* 4: 95–110.

Hoskins, W.G. (1955) *The Making of the English Landscape*, London: Hodder & Stoughton.

Hough, M. (1984) *City Form and Natural Process*, London and Sydney: Croom Helm.

Howett, C. (1987) 'Systems, signs and sensibilities', *Landscape Journal* 6, 1: 1–12.

Hunt, J.D. (1992) *Gardens and the Picturesque: studies in the history of landscape architecture*, Cambridge, MA: MIT Press.

Hussey, C. (1927) *The Picturesque: studies in a point of view*, New York: Putnam and Sons.

Jackson, J.B. (1979) 'The order of a landscape', in D.W. Meinig (ed.), *The Interpretation of Ordinary Landscapes*, Oxford: Oxford University Press.

Jackson, J.B. (1984) *Discovering the Vernacular Landscape*, New Haven: Yale University Press.

Jacobs, J. (1961) *The Life and Death of Great American Cities*, Harmondsworth: Penguin Books.

Jellicoe, G.A., Jellicoe, S. (1987) *The Landscape of Man*, London: Thames & Hudson.

Kaplan, S., Kaplan, R. (1982) *Humanscapes: environments for people*, Michigan: Ulrich Books.

Kaplan, R., Kaplan, S. (1989) *The Experience of Nature: a psychological perspective*, Cambridge: Cambridge University Press.

Lassus, B. (1998) *The Landscape Approach*, Philadelphia: University of Pennsylvania Press.

Laurie, I.C. (ed.) (1979) *Nature in Cities: the natural environment in the design and development of urban green space*, Chichester: Wiley.

Lowenthal, D. (1985) *The Past is a Foreign Country*, Cambridge: Cambridge University Press.

Mabbutt, J.A. (1968) 'Review of concepts of land classification', in G.A. Stewart, *Land Evaluation: papers of a CSIRO symposium, with UNESCO*, Melbourne: Macmillan.

Marsden, T., Murdoch, J., Lowe, P., Munton, R., Flynn, A. (1993) *Constructing the Countryside*, London: UCL Press.

Matless, D. (1998) *Landscape and Englishness*, London: Reaktion.

McHarg, I. (1969) *Design with Nature*, New York: Doubleday.

Meinig, D.W. (1979) 'The beholding eye: ten versions of the same scene', in D.W. Meinig (ed.), *The Interpretation of Ordinary Landscapes*, Oxford: Oxford University Press.

Meyer, E. (1994) 'Landscape architecture as modern other and postmodern ground', in H. Edquist and V. Bird (eds), *The Culture of Landscape Architecture*, Melbourne: RMIT.

Mitchell, W.J.T. (ed.) (1994) *Landscape and Power*, Chicago: University of Chicago Press.

Naveh, Z., Lieberman, R. (1994) *Landscape Ecology: theory and application*, New York: Springer Verlag.

Olwig, K. (2002) *Landscape, Nature, and the Body Politic*, Madison, WI: University of Wisconsin Press.

Oxford English Dictionary (1978) Oxford: Oxford University Press.

Relph, E. (1976) *Place and Placelessness*, London: Pion.

Relph, E. (1981) *Rational Landscapes and Humanistic Geography*, London: Croom Helm.

Relph, E. (1987) *The Modern Urban Landscape*, Baltimore: Johns Hopkins University Press.

Roberts, G. (1994) 'The cultural landscape', *Landscape Research* 19, 3:133–6.

Rose, G. (1993) *Feminism and Geography: the limits of geographical knowledge*, Cambridge: Polity.

Ruff, A. (1979) *Holland and the Ecological Landscapes*, Stockport, Cheshire: Deanwater Press.

Ruff, A., Tregay, R. (1982) 'An ecological approach to urban landscape design', *Occasional Paper No 8*, Manchester: Department of Town and Country Planning, University of Manchester.

Rybczynski, W. (1999) *A Clearing in the Distance: Frederick Law Olmsted and North America in the nineteenth century*, Toronto: Harper Collins.

Sauer, C.O. (1967) 'The morphology of landscape', in J. Leighly (ed.), *Land and Life*, Berkeley: University of California Press.

Seamon, D. (ed.) (1993) *Dwelling, Seeing, Designing*, Albany, NY: SUNY Press.

Seddon, G. (1994) *Searching for the Snowy: an environmental history*, St Leonards, NSW: Allen & Unwin.

Seddon, G. (1997) *Landprints: reflections on place and landscape*, Cambridge: Cambridge University Press.

Smith, B. (1960) *European Vision and the South Pacific 1768–1850*, Melbourne: Oxford University Press.

Smith, B. (1992) *Imaging the Pacific: in the wake of Cook's voyages*, Melbourne: Oxford University Press.

Soons, J.M., Selby, M.T. (1982) *The Landforms of New Zealand*, Auckland: Longman Paul.

Spirn, A.W. (1984) *The Granite Garden: urban nature and human design*, New York: Basic Books.

Spirn, A.W. (1998) *The Language of Landscape*, New Haven: Yale University Press.

Stilgoe, J.R. (1982) *Common Landscapes of America 1580–1845*, New Haven: Yale University Press.

Strang, G. (1998) 'Infrastructure as landscape', *Places* 10, 3: 8–15.

Swaffield, S.R. (2002) *Theory in Landscape Architecture: a reader*, Philadelphia: Pennsylvania University Press.

Swaffield, S.R., O'Connor, K.F. (1986) *Conceiving, Perceiving, Protecting and Using New Zealand Landscape Systems*, Christchurch, New Zealand: Centre for Resource Management, Lincoln University.

Thompson, G.F., Steiner, F.R. (eds) (1997) *Ecological Planning and Design*, New York: Wiley.

Thompson, I.H. (1999) *Ecology, Community and Delight*, London: E. & F.N. Spon.

Treib, M. (1993) *Modern Landscape Architecture: a critical review*, Cambridge, MA: MIT Press.

Tuan, Y.F. (1977) *Space and Place*, Minneapolis: University of Minnesota Press.

Tunnard, C. (1939) *Gardens in the Modern Landscape*, London: Architectural Press.

Turner, T.H.D. (1982–3) 'Landscape planning: a linguistic and historical analysis of the term's use', *Landscape Planning*, 9: 179–92.

Turner, T.H.D. (1996) *City as Landscape*, London: E. & F.N. Spon.

Urry. J. (1990) *The Tourist Gaze*, London: Sage.

Whyte, W. (1980) *The Social Life of Small Urban Spaces*, Washington, DC: Conservation Foundation.

Williams, R. (1960) *Border Country*, London: Chatto & Windus.

Williams, R. (1973) *The Country and the City*, London: Hogarth Press.

Chapter 2

Music-makers and the dreamers of dreams

John Hopkins

> We are the music-makers,
> And we are the dreamers of dreams,
> Wandering by lone sea-breakers,
> And sitting by desolate streams;
> World-losers and world-forsakers,
> On whom the pale moon gleams;
> Yet we are the movers and shakers
> Of the world for ever, it seems.

Arthur O'Shaughnessy

Introduction

Landscape is a human construct. We know its etymological derivation: originally the Old English noun *land* to which was added the suffix *scape*, 'landscape' became an abstract noun. Resurrected by the Dutch to construe the *ideal* place represented in a painting, it was then co-opted by English landscape designers to mean an *ideal* place.[1] In his remarkable essay *The Beholding Eye*, D. W. Meinig explores an extended definition of landscape through an analysis of the various ways in which we view landscape and the complexities of the human relation to it.[2] He crystallises how the landscape is freighted with competing views:

... there are those who look out upon that variegated scene and see landscape as ...

Nature: amidst all this man is minuscule, superficial, ephemeral, subordinate

Habitat: what we see before us is man continuously working at a viable relationship with nature

Artifact: the earth is a platform, but all thereon is furnished with man's effects so extensively that you cannot find a scrap of pristine nature

System: such a mind sees a river not as a river, but as a link in the hydrologic circuit

Problem: the evidence looms in almost any view: eroded hills, flooding rivers, shattered woods

Wealth: the eyes of an appraiser, assigning a monetary value to everything in view

Ideology: the whole scene as a symbol of values, the governing ideas, the underlying philosophies of a culture

History: a complex cumulative record of nature and man

Place: every landscape is a locality, an individual piece in the infinitely varied mosaic of the earth

Aesthetic: that there is something close to the essence, of beauty and truth, in the landscape.

Landscape, then, has powerful physical, environmental, economic, cultural, psychological and aesthetic components. Most importantly, it is what sustains us – our habitat – and it is nothing less than essential to our well-being, be it wild, naturalised, rural, suburban or urban. Landscape is the context for our lives and our livelihood. It is where we dwell, where we may live economists' notion of 'the good life'. The standard definition of economics is 'the study of the allocation of scarce means among competing ends'. The *means* is the use of natural resources and the power of labour to the *ends* of consumption, health, education, comfort, etc. – in other words, 'the good life'.

Bill Clinton, former president of the United States, recognised the economy as the foundation for political success when, during his first presidential election campaign, he reputedly stuck a scribbled 'Post-it' note to his bathroom mirror saying: 'It's the economy stupid!' Al Gore, Clinton's vice-president, recognised the environment, the landscape, as the baseline for the economy and wrote a powerful book, *Earth in Balance: Forging a New Common Purpose*, setting out his vision for a global Marshall plan that 'must, like the original, focus on strategic goals and emphasise actions and programs that are likely to remove the bottlenecks presently inhibiting the healthy functioning of the global economy'.[3]

Because the landscape is critical to our survival and to living the good life, we need powerful arguments to justify our manipulation of the landscape, asking fundamental questions such as: What right do we have to intervene in a landscape, and for what purpose? How is it sanctioned? What are the limits to our interventions? And when we do intervene, how do we measure what is 'good' or 'bad'? Who decides?

All these are questions of ethics. Ethics is the foundation for our system of values that dictate our actions towards others and towards the landscape, the environment. Ethics is concerned with how our personal moral codes connect with other individuals' codes and society's at large in such a way that we can live the good life. Ethics, put simply, is about what is right and what is wrong. Ethics provides the philosophical and intellectual basis for our actions – theory put into practice. It is the foundation of politics, economics and definitions of the good life. It is only through sound, powerful ethical arguments that we can answer the questions posed above about our rights to intervene in the landscape, the limits and nature of our interventions, and what is good or bad and who decides. We need to articulate and absorb an *environmental ethic* that underpins and runs through all we do as landscape architects and, indeed, human beings; an environmental ethic that is holistic, addressing economics and politics in addition to ecology, community and art, in service of the good life.

Ecology, community and art

This essay follows that in Jan Birksted's *Relating Architecture to Landscape,* where I argued for a philosophy of landscape architecture based on a triadic relationship between ecology, community and art.[4] The following is an abstract setting the context for this essay, which expands this philosophy to include the political economy.

All professions dealing with the environment are concerned with the creation of Utopia. Landscape architects, architects, planners, engineers, ecologists, economists, sociologists, biologists – the list goes on – all respond to the basic human urge to create our own Garden of Eden. Creating landscapes within which we can work, play, live and learn – creating the good life – is at the core of all we strive for. As D. W. Meinig, in distilling the writings of J. B. Jackson on the American landscape, wrote:

> In the broadest view, all landscapes are symbolic, every 'landscape is a reflection of the society which first brought it into being and

It is this role of the 'artist as interpreter' that necessitates as full an understanding as possible of the *genius loci* – the 'spirit of place' – which encompasses physical, historical, cultural and philosophical dimensions. With such a philosophical background, a Utopia based on ecology, community and art becomes a possibility. And, if we accept landscape architecture as an art; accept art as the manifestation of the collective cultural, historical and philosophical identity of a community (the *genius loci*); and accept that art is not only a sign of a unified society, but also a contributory factor in its creation, then the importance of landscape architecture through the 21st century is assured.

Ethics and the political economy

In attempting to answer the questions about our right to intervene in the landscape, this chapter goes on to describe the historical development of ethics, the emergence of human and environmental rights, and the development of environmental ethics. It goes on to describe how environmental ethics and ecology provide the framework for a new political economy that is supportive of sustainable development. It then briefly describes the emergence and application of environmental ethics through the planning system in the United Kingdom. It concludes with a manifesto for landscape architecture based on a new political economy, and for landscape architects to be directly involved at every level.

The historical development of ethics

In formulating and articulating an environmental ethics it is important to understand the concepts of human rights that emerged during the Enlightenment and the Industrial Revolution, and their subsequent application to human rights, the environment, politics and economics. We live in a world that is dominated by a philosophy derived from the Enlightenment of the 18th century. The Enlightenment led to:

- rational science replacing received religion;
- the perception of humanity changing from that of a series of communities to collectives of individuals;
- scientific knowledge and new forms of energy powering technological advances in the exploitation of humans, animals and the environment; and
- the establishment of our global, liberal, free-market economic system.

Several key historical figures link the western tradition of ethics.[14] Aristotle argued that we are social and rational animals and should, therefore, live virtuous lives, controlling our feelings and acting rationally. This only applied, however, to the Greek elite. In the 18th century, David Hume and Jean-Jacques Rousseau argued that morality was essentially a matter of feeling; but the question then was *whose* feelings take precedence, and how do we agree which feelings are right? Hume argued from the basic premise that humans are innately good, that we each have a love and benevolence for all humankind, and that this is what gives us common ground. In contrast, Kant argued that ethics was divorced from personal interests and desires and was based on universal laws – therefore, acting merely for the good of ourselves or others is no moral justification, we must derive ethical principles through abstract reasoning. Kant's moral philosophy is harsh and neglected real issues of human happiness or any discussion of the notion of 'the good life'. It did, however, establish the principle of universality.

After Kant, a number of British philosophers (notably Jeremy Bentham and John Stuart Mill), argued for an ethics that quite simply achieved the greatest good for the greatest number of people – morality was a question of utility. Ethics was the search for a 'personally satisfying life'.[15] John Stuart Mill spoke of the ultimate end of human action as being 'an existence exempt as far as possible from pain, and as rich as possible in enjoyments, both in point of quantity and quality'. He accepted that a balance needed to be struck to ensure that this end should be 'to the greatest extent possible, secured to all mankind; and not only to them, but, insofar as the nature of things admits, to the whole sentient creation'.[16] Utilitarianism was, therefore, an ethical basis for the good life that extended not only to humans but to *all* life. J. S. Mill's philosophy continues to influence contemporary ideas on environmental ethics and sustainability.

In the last century Jean-Paul Sartre argued that 'Man is nothing else but that which he makes himself'; in other words we each, individually, choose our own morality. As adults we are free to choose our own morality. However, our parents, our community, our professions and the state all have a vested interest in ensuring that we agree and share common moral codes. Through family, education and experience, we all shape our own morality. Sartre's approach is essentially self-centred and eschews a common bond. It takes to extremes the western individualist ethic enshrined in liberal, free-market, capitalist economics of the Industrial Revolution, which were revivified in the Reagan/Thatcher era.

Ayn Rand was an ethical egoist. Her book *The Fountainhead* (and the film of the same name starring Gregory Peck) was about an individualist architect struggling for his new 'modern' forms against the Beaux Arts norm. It was published in 1943 and influenced a generation of Modernist architects.

She believed that we always ought to act in our own interest. The opposite of egoism is altruism, which is acting for the sake of other people's interests: do unto others as you would have them do unto you. There are inevitable tensions between acting for oneself and acting for others. In a series of seminal sermons published in 1726, Bishop Joseph Butler concluded that there is an element of each in all our actions, and that they can be in harmony – our actions are always both for others and ourselves.

In terms of contemporary ethics, Harvard professor and Pulitzer-winning author Edward O. Wilson believes that:

> We are entering a new era of existentialism, not the old absurdist existentialism of Kierkegaard and Sartre, giving complete autonomy to the individual, but the concept that only unified learning, universally shared, makes accurate foresight and wise choice possible. In the course of it all we are learning the fundamental principle that ethics is everything. Human social existence, unlike animal sociality, is based on genetic propensity to form long-term contracts that evolve by culture into moral precepts and law.[17]

Ethics then, is the meta-construct for everyday human existence.

The emergence of human rights and environmental ethics

Some scholars see the rudiments of human rights in Stoic philosophy and *ius naturale* of Roman law; however, their true origins are found in the English, American and French revolutions of the 17th and 18th centuries.[18] The English Bill of Rights of 1689 laid down rules about the liberties and rights of individuals. The American Declaration of Independence of 1776 enshrined the right to life, liberty and the pursuit of happiness. Individual rights included in the US Bill of Rights of 1791 were incorporated into the Constitution through amendments which guaranteed, *inter alia*, freedom of religion, of the press and of the right to assembly, protection against unreasonable search and seizure, etc.

The Industrial Revolution was a further, integral spur to the emergence of human rights. No longer was the weaver-worker semi-autonomous, with a garden and/or common land to which they could turn for a critical part of their living. The emergence of the machine and factories and the enclosure of land in England (in the name of efficiency) changed that economy dramatically. Individuals were now reliant solely on their own labour, but only when and if the factory owner needed it. Labour was commodified. If there was no work, God or nature could no longer be blamed – industrialised society could be, and was.[19] The view of the human as an individual with rights spurred the battles for individual freedom, rights and democratic control that continue today. It was an immense upheaval driven by technological advances, appalling living conditions and abuse of power.

The French Revolution, following the course set by the English and American ones, spawned the Declaration of the Rights of Man and the Citizen (1789). Article 4 states:

> Liberty consists in being able to do anything that does not harm others; thus the exercise of the natural rights of every man has no bounds other than those that ensure to the other members of society the enjoyment of these same rights. Only Law may determine these bounds.

The principles and concepts that originated in the English, American and French revolutions are threefold: that rights are by their nature 'inherent, universal and inalienable – they belong to the individuals simply because they are human beings and not because they are the subjects of a state's law'; that those rights are best protected through a democratic framework; and that limits to the exercise of those rights could 'only be determined or abrogated by law'.[20]

Karel Vasak has argued that the continuing historical development of human rights can be classified according to the French revolutionary slogan 'Liberty, equality and fraternity'. The first-generation rights concerning liberty are about individual civil and political liberties. The second generation concerning equality correspond to economic, social and cultural rights to fulfil individual potential – under these rights, it is incumbent on the state to put in place programmes to allow this. The third-generation rights concerning fraternity 'are the newest and most controversial category of rights. These are asserted, in particular, by developing states which wish to see the creation of an international and legal and economic order that will guarantee the right to development, to disaster relief assistance, to peace and to a *good environment*.'[21] (Emphasis added.) This is the nascence of environmental ethics.

The development of an environmental ethics

With the establishment of the League of Nations and the United Nations in the aftermath of the First and Second World Wars, respectively, the Allies saw a commitment to the protection of human rights as a 'prerequisite to the creation of a just and stable international order'.[22] Civil, political, economic, social and cultural rights became enshrined in the Universal Declaration of Human Rights. The emergence of the declaration also traces that of an environmental ethics and consequent ideas of sustainable development.

The UN General Assembly sought to give the Declaration of Human Rights a legal status and to provide institutions and mechanisms for supervision and enforcement. This led to two separate covenants: the International Covenant on Civil and Political Rights (ICCPR) and the International Covenant on Economic, Social and Cultural Rights (ICESCR). (Although these were ready for signature in 1966, they did not come into force until 1976.) The UN Human Rights Committee was established to supervise the implementation of the ICCPR, which provided for the protected rights to be respected and ensured immediately, whereas the ICESCR provided for the states to merely 'recognise' the rights contained in the covenant and implement them progressively in accordance with specific programmes.[23] The ICESCR contains the right to 'a good environment'.

There were, perhaps, three turning points in *popular* recognition of the need for a holistic environmental ethics: major pollution caused by industry; the photographs of the earth seen from the moon taken by Apollo 11 in 1969; and the oil crisis of 1973. The first was a palpable indication of degradation of the environment and of human health – air pollution, oil spills, pesticides, etc; the second a humbling view of the beauty, vulnerability and isolation of the earth – it is, indeed, our spaceship, with nothing to sustain us other than finite natural resources and the transforming energy of the sun; the third made it clear how much we were dependant on 'cheap' stored energy of the sun in the form of oil.

In 1972, the United Nations Conference on the Human Environment in Stockholm established the United Nations Environment Programme (UNEP) to coordinate global environmental initiatives. In 1980 the UNEP along with the International Union for Nature Conservation and Natural Resources (IUCN) and the World Wide Fund for Nature (WWF) published the *World Conservation Strategy*. It was the first document to use the term 'sustainable development'. The three fundamental principles were: 1) essential ecological processes and life-support systems must be maintained, 2) genetic diversity must be preserved, and 3) any use of species or ecosystems must be sustainable. The UN-sponsored World (Brundtland) Commission on the Environment and Development in 1987 refined the definition of sustainable development as 'development that meets the needs of the present without compromising the ability of future generations to meet their own needs'. In 1987 the UNEP, again in conjunction with the IUCN and WWF, published *Caring for the Earth: A Strategy for Sustainable Living*, which gave more extended definitions of sustainable development.

In 1992, the Earth Summit in Rio de Janeiro committed signatories to the preservation of biodiversity and to controlling climate change through reduction in pollution emissions. It was recognised that this had to be driven at the community level through *Local Agenda 21*. It charged every government to take into account the social, economic and environmental well-being of all of its citizens (summed up in the mantra 'think global, act local') and established the *precautionary* principle in relation to development and to protection of the environment:

> In order to protect the environment, the precautionary approach shall be widely applied by States according to their capabilities. Where there are threats of serious or irreversible damage, lack of full scientific certainty shall not be used as a reason for postponing cost-effective measures to prevent environmental degradation.[24]

In other words, protection of the environment should be paramount, scientific rationalism tempered.

However, the political, economic and environmental objectives of the Rio Summit were not achieved. In September 2002, the World Summit on Sustainable Development in Johannesburg, which was intended to reinvigorate Rio, also failed. As Kofi Annan, Secretary General of the United Nations, noted, 'Unsustainable approaches to economic progress remain pervasive.'[25] It is clear, therefore, that a new global political economic system needs to be fashioned on the basis of a global environmental ethic. The data remain compelling. The following paragraphs give a snapshot of the state of the world in 2002 given in a publication of the World Watch Institute.[26]

Consumption and energy

Consumption and production levels, based on the global average ecological footprint, were 25 per cent higher than the earth's ecological capacity. This means that even at 2001 levels humanity is eroding the planet's natural capital at a significant rate. World energy consumption had increased significantly since 1992 and was expected to grow at a rate of 2 per cent a year until 2020. Global consumption of fossil fuels had increased by 10 per cent from 1992 to 1999, and per capita use remained highest in developed countries, where people consumed up to 6.5 tonnes of oil equivalent per year, ten times the consumption in developing countries. Governments in all countries subsidised inefficient and unsustainable uses of energy and transport, at a cost of between $650 billion and $1.5 trillion a year. Twenty per cent of the existing global demand for oil and gas was in Asia, and even more importantly, more than 50 per cent of the growth in demand each year comes from that region. If the global growth rate of about 2 per cent a year for primary energy use continues, it will mean a doubling of energy consumption by 2035 relative to 1998, and a tripling by 2055. There have been no major oil or gas finds since the early 1990s.

Water, sanitation and health

Some 1.1 billion people, or 18 per cent of the world's population, lacked access to safe drinking water, and over 2.4 billion people lacked access to adequate sanitation. More than 2.2 million people in developing countries, most of them children, died each year from diseases associated with lack of access to safe drinking water, inadequate sanitation and poor hygiene. A large proportion of people in developing countries suffered from diseases caused either directly or indirectly by the consumption of contaminated water or food or by disease-carrying organisms that breed in water. In developing countries, between 90 and 95 per cent of sewage and 70 per cent of industrial wastes were dumped untreated into waters where they pollute the usable water supply. Between five and six million people in developing countries died each year from waterborne diseases and air pollution. Poor environmental quality contributed to 25 per cent of all preventable illness in the world today. In the year 2000, 1.3 million children aged under five in developing countries died from diarrhoeal diseases caused by unsafe water supply, inadequate sanitation and poor hygiene.

The environment

Desertification affected almost a quarter of the world's total land area, and almost 70 per cent of the world's dry lands face further degradation. Often caused by overgrazing and overuse of marginal land, and closely linked with rural poverty and hunger, desertification threatened the livelihoods of over one billion people in 100 countries. Since 1991, the world has lost a net total of some 94 million hectares of forest, an area larger than Venezuela. The rate of deforestation was highest in developing countries in tropical areas, where 4 per cent of the region's forests were lost over the last decade. Human activity had degraded more than half of the world's coastal ecosystems. For Europe the figure was 80 per cent and for Asia 70 per cent. Sea levels have risen 10–20 cm since 1900, most non-polar glaciers were retreating, and the extent and thickness of Arctic Sea ice was decreasing, according to the Intergovernmental Panel on Climate Change. It found that about 46 million people per year experience flooding caused by storm surges. A 50 cm rise in the sea level would increase this number to about 92 million, and a rise of a metre would increase this number to 118 million.

Fisheries provided direct and indirect livelihoods for some 400 million people. More than a quarter of the world's fisheries were over-utilised and half were exploited at full capacity. Overall, 75 per cent of the world's fisheries required immediate steps to freeze or reduce fishing to ensure a future supply of fish. It was predicted that crop yields in Africa could drop by half if soil degradation continues at the present rate. Almost 65 per cent of agricultural lands had already been affected.

A new global economics based on ethics and ecology

The evidence that our current global economic system is effectively divorced from our environmental base is clear. No less a figure than Joseph Stiglitz, a former chief economist of the World Bank, has documented the negative effects of a global economy that uncritically accepts the free movement of capital, which is dominated by global businesses beyond the sanction even of national governments, and in which, despite unprecedented economic growth from 1991 to 2001, adding over $10 trillion a year to the global economy, the number of people living in poverty declined only slightly, from about 1.3 billion to 1.2 billion.[27] As Edward O. Wilson has noted, 'The single greatest intellectual obstacle to environmental realism, as opposed to practical difficulty, is the myopia of most professional economists.'[28] The establishment of a new political economy that is based on the principles of ecology and informed by an environmental ethics is, and will continue to be, the centre ground of political debate through the early decades of the 21st century. The following sections mark out the territory for that debate.

Ecology

Crucial to the emergence of an environmental ethics has been and remains the discipline of ecology. The science of ecology is essentially a 20th-century one. The term was coined in 1866 by the German biologist Ernst Haeckel from the Greek words *oikos*, meaning 'house' or 'place to live', and *logos*, meaning 'study of'. It is now accepted as 'the study of the relationships among living organisms and to the totality of physical and biological factors making up their environment'.[29] It is, therefore, a holistic science that crosses disciplinary boundaries; it is about connectedness, wholeness. Out of ecology came the notion of self-sustaining collections of organisms within their environment.

These are known as ecological systems or ecosystems, a term first introduced by the English botanist A. G. Tansley in 1935. And out of an understanding of ecosystems came the notion of economic sustainability.

As noted earlier, landscape architecture, as a cross-disciplinary activity concerned with the human *and* natural environment and the relationship between the two, is well placed to emerge as one of the most important professions of the 21st century. The notion of sustainable development, of stewardship, is adumbrated in all definitions of landscape architecture. My argument for a paradigm of landscape architecture based on ecology, community and art requires a paradigm shift in political-economic philosophy.[30]

The scientific rationale is relatively simple. We live on a planet that has a finite amount of matter that, according to the law of conservation of matter, cannot be created or destroyed. In other words, what we have on earth is all there is, and we cannot throw any of it away; there will always be pollution of some sort. The question of what is an acceptable level of pollution is an ethical one. The first law of thermodynamics similarly states that energy cannot be created or destroyed. When a rock falls to the ground, the potential energy of the rock is converted into kinetic energy as it falls. The friction between the rock and the air it passes through and of the particles of soil when it hits the ground means that all its energy has been merely transferred. Energy input always equals energy output. The second law of thermodynamics is the law of energy degradation: as energy is used up it goes from a usable form to a less usable form. This is also known as entropy, the tendency for a system towards randomness and disorder. When oil (concentrated, low-entropy energy) is burned, it is reduced to relatively unusable heat energy (dissipated, high-entropy energy). And once used, that is it. The question of how quickly we should use up low-entropy, usable energy is another ethical one.

Economics

Economics has the same etymological root as ecology and literally means 'household management'. As noted earlier, the standard definition of economics is 'the study of the allocation of scarce means among competing ends' with the aim of achieving 'the good life'. Classical, free-market, liberal economics, rooted firmly in Enlightenment philosophies, has developed without reference to the environment. Based on unending 'growth', it classifies the individual as the base economic unit to the detriment of communities. And, as noted above, it is now global in nature and beyond the control even of democratically elected national governments.

We therefore need to think in terms of and redefine the 'ultimate end' of economic activity – the good life – on the basis of ecology and informed by an environmental ethics. Inevitably, the definition of the ultimate end is directly linked to the ultimate means to achieve that end. The means is the environment, which presents biophysical limits. The *only* arguments in deciding whether we continue to use up the earth's non-renewable resources in an orgy of consumption or whether we take account of the needs of future generations are ethical ones based on a redefinition of ultimate ends and ultimate means.

Herman Daly has consistently argued for an economic paradigm based on ecology and ethics. He says, 'The overall problem is how to use Ultimate Means to serve best the Ultimate End. We might call this *ultimate political economy*, or *stewardship*.'[31] He and John Cobb argue for a new economics that is not based solely on the currently accepted classical and neo-classical paradigm that defines every political-economic argument as right, centre or left wing, anarchist, social democratic or fascist. They argue for an economics based on communities and on communities of communities, starting with neighbourhoods and finishing with the world community. They cite the European Community as a good, yet imperfect, example of a community of communities, working together within a world community. (Imperfections relate to, among many others, over-centralisation and concentration of power, and lack of democratic accountability.) The ultimate end of community-based economics is as much to provide 'meaningful and personally satisfying work as to provide adequate goods and services'.[32] This is the good life based on an environmental ethic. Daly agrees that a precise definition of the good life is not an easy task, but that as a starting point 'most would agree with Malthus that it should be such as to permit one to have a glass of wine and a piece of meat with one's dinner'. He goes on: 'Even if one is a teetotaller or a vegetarian that level of affluence is desirable.'[33]

It is clear that the continued industrialisation of the world economy and of 'undeveloped' economies cannot continue, because it is based on 'large scale, factory-style energy and capital intensive, specialised production units that are hierarchically managed, and that rely heavily on non-renewable resources and waste absorption capacities at non-sustainable rates'.[34] The true costs of production must be taken into account, including human, community and environmental costs, in terms of resource depletion and pollution. Unfortunately, as described above, globalisation of the economy works against this happening.

Globalisation continues apace with agreements such as the General Agreement on Tariffs and Trade (GATT). The World Trade Organization has great global power – greater than the United Nations – but no environmental mandate or constraints. The free movement of capital without reference to environmental concerns needs to be undermined on the grounds of sustainability. The vast majority of contemporary governments subscribe to the predominant classical liberal economic system and are committed to economic growth without constraints imposed by the biophysical limits of the earth. Economic growth is their first and, seemingly, only priority. If those governments set environmental and social standards that international corporations view as too onerous, those corporations invest elsewhere. Governments, therefore, oblige themselves to comply with international corporate demands, even to the extent of offering competitive loans to encourage investment in their country rather than another. The free movement of global capital exacerbates environmental and social problems. Jobs in one community that acts responsibly with regard to sustainable production of goods and services can be moved to another community that has lower or no standards, and thus those goods and services can be provided much more cheaply.

The *maquiladora* industries south of Mexico's border with the United States are a classic example. There, Mexican industry produces goods for export to the US without having to meet the same environmental or employment standards.[35] Daly suggests a system of tariffs to resolve this.[36] The tariffs would tend to equalise one community's choices on wage levels, welfare, resource use and pollution with another's, and in so doing encourage self-sufficiency and sustainable development.

One of the most important economic questions that needs to be addressed is that of biophysical limits on the scale of the world economy. Quite simply, this should be determined by the scale of community economies, which are themselves determined by biophysical limits – the *environmental carrying capacity* of the community's hinterland. (Environmental carrying capacity is determined by the amount of renewable resources that the ecosystem can sustain, and how much waste it can absorb.) The scale of the economy can, therefore, be measured as the number of people times the per capita rates of resource use. Herman Daly and John Cobb define in some detail the economic measures and parameters of a sustainable economic system in *For the Common Good*.[37]

Mathis Wackman and William Rees have developed the notion of 'ecological footprints' – the measure of material and energy flows required to support communities. For example, London's surface area is 390,000 acres. To support London's community the farmland required (at 3 acres/person) is 21 million acres; the forest area required for wood products needed (at 0.27 acres/person) is 1.9 million acres; the land area required for carbon absorption (at 3.7 acres/person) is 26 million acres. These figures give a total ecological footprint of 48.9 million acres – 125 times London's surface area.[38] If everyone in the world were to live like an average person in the high-income countries, we would need 2.6 additional planets to support us all.[39] Ghandi simplified this even further and with typical prescience in saying, 'There is enough for everyone's need, but not for everyone's greed.'

Natural capitalism

In their remarkable book *Natural Capitalism*, Paul Hawkens and Amory and Hunter Lovins set out a manifesto for the 'next industrial revolution'.[40] It has been heralded by the former US president Bill Clinton as essential reading; seminars have been given at 10 Downing Street. As the title suggests, it proposes a 'capitalism' based on nature and the following principles:

- the environment is not a minor factor of production but rather is an envelope containing, provisioning and sustaining the entire economy;
- the limiting factor to future economic development is the availability and functionality of natural capital, in particular, life-supporting services that have no substitutes and currently have no market value;
- misconceived or badly designed business systems, population growth and wasteful patterns of consumption are the primary causes of the loss of natural capital, and all three must be addressed to achieve a sustainable economy;
- future economic progress can best take place in democratic, market-based systems of production and distribution in which all forms of capital are fully valued, including human, manufactured, financial and natural capital;
- one of the keys to the most beneficial employment of people, money and the environment is radical increases in resource productivity;
- human welfare is best served by improving the quality and flow of desired services delivered, rather than merely increasing the total dollar flow;
- economic and environmental sustainability depends on redressing global inequities of income and material well-being; and
- the best long-term environment for commerce is provided by true democratic systems of governance that are based on the needs of people rather than business.[41]

The way to achieve 'natural capitalism', the authors believe, is by:

- imitating nature in production processes – 'biomimicry' – so that waste is virtually eliminated through continuous cycles;

- reducing resource consumption and increasing resource productivity by 90 per cent;
- shifting the emphasis of the economy away from goods and purchases to one of *services* and *flows*; and
- by investment in natural capital so that our ecosystems provide more services and natural resources.

Landscape architects have a key role to play in this revolution. We can promote and influence policies through design proposals that:

- are 'designed with nature and the community', protecting and enhancing natural capital;
- reduce capital and energy resource consumption;
- eliminate waste and promote recycling;
- encourage high-quality, high-density towns and cities that reduce private car use and increase use of public transport;
- encourage agricultural practices that enhance soil fertility, biodiversity and production; and
- create 'working landscapes' that are beautiful, functioning places that people connect with, take responsibility for and enjoy living, working and playing in.

There are some encouraging signs in the reorientation of economies to sustainable development. During the 1980s and 1990s, of the developed nations Germany, Japan, The Netherlands, Norway and Sweden scored highly in terms of the amount of energy required to produce a unit of national income, low per capita emissions of pollutants and low per capita generation of household garbage and other solid wastes. They all have strong environmental legislation, but more importantly, according to John Dryzek, professor of politics at the University of Melbourne, in *The Politics of the Earth*, 'What these countries have in common is a political-economic system where consensual relationships among key actors prevail.'[42]

Politics

The establishment of 'community-scaled economies' related to biophysical limits, as proposed by Daly and Cobb, also requires corresponding devolution of political powers. As they point out, 'a political community cannot be healthy if it cannot exercise a significant measure of control over its economic life'.[43] As a basic principle of sustainable development, power should be devolved to the smallest community units feasible – the European Community's 'subsidiarity' principle. In order to achieve this, our democratic systems need to be reinvigorated to ensure that members of the community take a much more active part in, and more responsibility for, decision-making.

Three approaches to changing local government in the UK and the US have been identified by Professor Robin Hambleton in his paper 'Future Directions for Urban Government in Britain and America':[44]

- the radical-right strategy of cutting public spending and promoting privatisation;
- the centre-left strategy of reforming public service to respond to needs of consumers; and
- the radical-liberal strategy of reform of public service to empower the consumer and the citizen in order to strengthen local democracy.

The last recognises that the idea of citizenship is far more complex than viewing individuals merely as consumers, and that they should be viewed much more as active participants in the creation and sustenance of community life.

The politics of what can be loosely described as the 'green movement' has been analysed by John Dryzek.[45] He rightly recognises that the issues are complex, interrelated and deal with the 'whole range of moral and aesthetic questions about human livelihood, human attitudes, and our proper relation to other entities on the planet'.[46] He has identified four main discourses that characterise political reactions and remedies to environmental problems.

The first he terms 'environmental problem solving', which is the response of the existing political-economic system. Through systems of incentives and disincentives (effectively putting prices on environmental benefits and disbenefits), environmental problems, it is argued, can be satisfactorily resolved. Environmental concern and expertise is, thus, institutionalised. The second he terms 'survivalism', which is a response to the early 1970s view of population and natural resource limits as apocalyptic. The only solution to these problems is through draconian, worldwide, authoritarian controls: 'Think globally, act globally.'[47] The third he terms 'sustainability', which recognises biophysical limits but works through a redefinition of the concepts of growth and development within a framework of sustainability. As we have seen, the Brundtland report of 1987 marks the beginning of the sustainability discourse, and Dryzek notes that 'more recently, ideas of ecological modernisation, seeing economic growth and environmental protection as essentially complementary, have arisen in Europe'.[48]

The fourth and final discourse he terms 'green radicalism', which he views as the 'most significant ideological development of the late twentieth century'.[49] This diverse discourse includes all the radical activists characterised by 'Swampy' (famous for his exploits in underground tunnelling to stop construction of the Newbury bypass in the UK) and the Seattle, Milan and Davos protestors at the World Trade Organization's annual summit meetings. It also extends to Green Party politicians, who have had some success in taking on established politics, particularly in Germany and, to a lesser extent, in London. He identifies two extremes of this movement: 'Green Romantics' and 'Green Rationalists', directly descended from the Romantics and the Rationalists of the Enlightenment period. Green Romantics believe in personal change but have no real view of how this can be achieved on the scale required to solve environmental problems. Green Rationalists, on the other hand, take part in *realpolitik* and, while they have neither a fully defined blueprint for a 'green' society nor a strategy of how to achieve it, they do have a plethora of ideas for moving towards it.

Dryzek concludes that ecological modernisation, allied with dispute resolution that is based on a revitalised participatory democracy, is an encouraging way forward. He terms this 'ecological democracy'.[50] As one example of this kind of radicalised democracy, he cites the inquiry carried out by Mr Justice Thomas Berger into the proposed construction of a pipeline carrying gas and oil from the Canadian Arctic:

> Berger took pains to make sure that resource-poor interests, especially indigenous peoples, were provided with funds, access to expertise, and an ability to testify in a forum under conditions with which they were familiar (the inquiry travelled to remote villages). He interpreted the terms of reference broadly, to encompass development strategies for the Canadian North, not just whether a pipeline should be built. In this sense, the inquiry became more like a policy dialogue. Berger's report ... proposes a reinvigorated renewable resource-based economy for the Canadian North, in which oil and gas development have little place. Berger pushed democratic pragmatism to its limits – and perhaps beyond – to the kind of participatory process favoured by green radicalism.[51]

Environmental ethics and the UK planning system

In 1800 the population of the UK was around 10.5 million and predominantly rural. Within 100 years, the population had soared to 37 million and was largely urban. The appalling living conditions created by this combination of population growth and urbanisation were addressed in the Public Health Act of 1875, inspired by public health reformer Edwin Chadwick.

The 1909 Housing and Town Planning Act and the 1919 Housing Act were followed in 1932 by the Town and Country Planning Act. This act introduced, for the first time, the concept of development control and of 'planning schemes'. The 1947 Town and Country Planning Act established the current framework for planning, requiring the preparation of development plans based on administrative areas. The 1947 Act established the principle that no development should take place without planning permission. The 1968 Act introduced, among other things, better provision for public participation. The development of the planning system was closely related to provisions for local government and, hence, for local democracy. A number of planning designations refer to 'landscape', from National Parks, Areas of Outstanding Natural Beauty and greenbelts to more local and biodiversity-oriented Sites of Special Scientific Interest and Sites of Interest for Nature Conservation. There are also a number of policy guidance notes (PPGs) that refer and relate to landscape and development, including PPG3 on housing and PPG17 on open space, sports and recreation.

In the UK, therefore, planning legislation has been the main statutory instrument defining and controlling physical development and is increasingly addressing environmental and community concerns. Its nascence and development reflect ethical concerns for public health, environmental protection and local democracy. The planning system essentially provides the framework and the forum for public debate of, and sanction for, our interventions in the landscape.

Through the 1980s and 1990s, the Thatcher and Major governments took, as with the economy and many other areas of public life, a *laisser-faire* attitude to planning. They believed in and relied on the 'market' to decide how best to build and where, and promoted and catered for the 'great car economy'. These almost two decades of *laisser-faire* planning left a legacy of low-density, low-quality suburbs with no sense of place or community, and a network of out-of-town shopping centres that make no contribution to community life. Meanwhile, inner cities in particular deteriorated into wastelands of neglect, poverty and dirt. Parks and open spaces, many of them bequeathed to us, paradoxically, by Victorian responses to the needs of communities, were also starved of capital and revenue resources to the point where many of them became no-go areas.

Since the 'New' Labour government came to power in 1997 there has been a consistent effort to redress the balance, to focus development within existing urban areas and/or on brownfield land and to improve quality of life. In response to the 1992 Rio de Janeiro Earth Summit's Agenda 21 initiative, it published *A Better Quality of Life: A Strategy for Sustainable Development in the United Kingdom*.[52] It also established the Sustainable Transport

Commission and the Sustainable Development Commission, the Urban Task Force and the Urban Green Spaces Task Force.

The Urban Task Force's report *Towards an Urban Renaissance*, commissioned by the government, recognised that 'an urban renaissance should be founded on the principles of design excellence, economic strength, environmental responsibility, good governance and social well-being'.[53] The report resulted in the government's *Urban White Paper*, the new Planning Bill, the Sustainable Communities Plan, the rewriting of all planning policy guidelines (now planning policy statements) and a plethora of design guides and good practice documents. It also resulted in the establishment of the Commission for Architecture and the Built Environment (CABE) – the government's advisory body on the built environment – which, in turn, has published much good guidance and raised public and political awareness of the benefits of good planning and design.

The report commissioned by the government from the Urban Green Spaces Task Force led to the publication of *Living Places: Cleaner, Safer, Greener* in October 2002. It drew together the work of six government departments, reflecting the cross-cutting nature of parks and the public realm, and recognised that 'the quality of our public spaces affects the quality of all our lives. It affects how we feel about where we live, where we work, and where our children play.'[54] It also led to the establishment of a new department within CABE, CABE Space, charged with championing 'the vital role of urban parks and green spaces in improving quality of life and delivering the urban renaissance'.[55]

The government's *Sustainable Communities Plan* promotes high-density, high-quality and energy-efficient developments on brownfield land (a target of 60 per cent of all new homes), supported by public transport systems. A target for affordable housing for rent and for sale, particularly for 'key workers' such as the police, doctors, nurses and teachers, is set at 40 per cent. These are all positive contributions in establishing the political parameters of sustainable development.

Additionally, the planning system itself has changed, after a new Planning Bill received royal assent in 2004. The intention of the new legislation is to:

- speed up the planning process;
- make it more responsive to communities' needs and aspirations; and
- convert it to a more pro-active, plan-led process through the adoption of local development frameworks and area development frameworks (both spatial plans).

It remains to be seen whether the almost mutually exclusive objectives of greater speed and community engagement will be achieved. Local authorities will have to prepare overarching 'community strategies' addressing economic, social and environmental issues. These are intended to be cross-cutting, pro-active and driven by communities' needs and aspirations. Policy formulation will, perhaps, become a bottom-up as well as a top-down process, with policy implementation the responsibility of an accountable council membership and executive. Additionally, through the publication of *Planning Policy Guidance 1: General policy and principles*, design quality and sustainability are now material considerations in planning applications.

In legislating for planning, therefore, the language and sentiment of government has, and is, moving in the right direction. It has addressed, and continues to address, social, economic and environmental issues in a coordinated way. However, there is never any doubt or dissent that the economy is the primary driver. And, despite all this activity, and despite the government's 1997 election commitment that the environment would be central to policy-making, over-arching legislation for sustainable development, allied with fiscal mechanisms to require it, has largely been absent, and significant progress scant.

Environmental ethics and local democracy

Along with planning legislation, the New Labour government was also keen to reform local government and democracy. Its proposed programme was published in 'Revitalising Local Democracy'.[56] Significantly, the legislation has placed a duty on councils to 'promote the economic, social and environmental well-being of their areas' and ensure that they 'at all times, consider the long-term well-being of their area'.[57] The impulse behind these changes is radical and long-term and derives directly from the Brundtland report. However, the mooted reforms to the 'first past the post' voting system are now long dead. The lack of broader introduction of proportional representation, and the opportunity this would afford to re-engage disenfranchised voters, has set back the local democracy agenda.

With an average turnout at local elections in the UK of just 40 per cent, the need for greater political engagement is self-evident. In 1998, one constituency in Liverpool recorded a voter turnout of just 9 per cent for a local election. This presents a very real threat to democracy and to the long-term viability and credibility of both local and national government. Many people are disenfranchised, disenchanted and disaffected. This democratic deficit has serious ramifications for the very notion of community and has led to a disinclination for people to engage with their community and to a decline in their trust of politicians. The consequent physical and psychological degradation in our communities is evident. What we need is to return a sense of belonging,

ownership, control, responsibility and mutuality to our communities through active citizenship. The decision-making process needs to be more transparent, responsive and accountable at a local level. Only then will people feel that voting counts and that it does make a difference and will understand how and why it is important.

The establishment of the Greater London Assembly and the election of a mayor (along with Green Party members under the rules of proportional representation) can only be viewed as a positive step towards regional government. The enabling legislation placed three duties on the Assembly 'to do anything' to promote in Greater London: economic development (note: not growth) and wealth creation; social development; and the improvement of the environment. In order to achieve this, the mayor has produced strategies for integrated transport, economic development, biodiversity, municipal waste management, air quality, ambient noise, spatial development, and culture. Additionally, each of the strategies has to be consistent with all the others. The Greater London Authority under Mayor Ken Livingstone is proving successful and could provide a model for other cities and communities.

We must continue to develop policies, programmes and initiatives that encourage people to become actively involved citizens. There is a certain schizophrenia in the way we currently make personal political and economic

2.1

Sutcliffe Park, London, was a barren recreation ground with the Quaggy River culverted underneath it. Our community organisation, the Quaggy Waterways Action Group, fought a flood alleviation proposal to widen, deepen and canalise the river. Over a 15-year period, we worked with the authorities to achieve this innovative transformation

2.2
Manor House
Gardens, London,
was a typically run-
down park. We
formed the User
Group in 1993 with
a vision to restore
it, and worked
(sometimes
battled) with the
authorities to
achieve a £1
million restoration
funded by the
Heritage Lottery
Fund. The
restoration was
completed in 2000,
and the park is now
at the heart of
community life
once more: clean,
safe, attractive and
beautiful

decisions. Yes, we want good public transport, schools, health service, parks, streets, etc., but we vote against the taxes necessary to pay for them. This lack of political trust should change as democratic decision-making is driven down to the appropriate community level. We may then see a merging of our 'individual' and our 'community' selves with decisions taken for the common good.

11 September 2001

No discussion of ethics, the environment, economics and sustainability – indeed, no discussion of anything on a global scale – can ignore the reality and the ramifications of the 11 September 2001 attack on the twin towers of the World Trade Center, New York, and the consequent war in Iraq. The events indicate how global politics, the economy and the environment are conjoined in an unstable world. There is also no doubt that the solutions to global political, economic and environmental instability lie not in waging war, but in striving for social, environmental and economic equity and justice.

In the UK, as New Labour's second term of office draws to a close, and despite many positive aspects, the feeling of 1997 – that the country might be about to enter a new era – has been lost. The New Labour government of 1997 did, at the time, seem to recognise a shift in the political landscape and attempted to address the increasing complexity of problems with some radical ideas under the rubric of 'joined-up' government. It was the correct response. However, their delivery on devolution, reform of the House of Lords, freedom of information, proportional representation, social exclusion, education, health care, decentralisation to the regions, transport, the environment and reform of local government all appear to be stymied by the rhetoric of classical, free-market, liberal economics, which remains their strongest and most compelling rationale.

Conclusion: a manifesto

From the 17th to the 20th century we can see the development of universally agreed individual and collective rights being extended and applied to the environment. These rights spring from an ethical foundation concerned with notions of the good life for individuals, the community *and* the environment.

In order to answer the question of what right we have to intervene in a landscape, our only recourse is to ethics. As landscape architects, our moral authority derives from: our personal ethics (family and friends); our cultural or civic ethics (the communities we live and work within and for); and government (in a democracy, sanctioned by the governed, and disseminated through fiscal and legislative policies and mechanisms that support national and global universal rights). As landscape architects, we must participate in the formulation and development of fiscal and legislative policies and mechanisms that are based on an environmental ethics. The definition of this environmental ethics must be holistic, cross-disciplinary and collaborative. It must be based on ecological, democratic and community principles. Strong communities are the prerequisite for political, economic, social, physical and psychological stability.

If we agree with Hume that humans are innately good, with Kant that there *are* universal ethical principles, and if we support the Universal Declaration of Human Rights and the United Nations Environment Programme, then we should support moves towards a political economy based on ecology and ethics – an ecological economics where definitions of the ultimate end (the good life) and the ultimate means (the environment) are limited by ethics and the biosphere respectively. We should call this 'stewardship', place it at the heart of development practice, and support:

- moves to put an end to the free movement of capital;
- the decentralisation of economic and political power to the most appropriate community level (subsidiarity);

2.3
West India Quay,
London (Tate Hopkins
Landscape Architects
and Planners) is a
prime example of the
successful re-use of
redundant docklands.
The warehouses,
listed Grade I by
English Heritage,
now house the
London Museum of
Docklands.
Apartments, shops,
restaurants and
cafes spill out
onto the dockside,
which accommodates
urban events such
as the Seafood
Festival, illustrated
here

- a much more open, participatory and transparent democracy;
- the development of the planning system to reflect environmental, economic and community needs more; and
- more fiscal and legislative mechanisms promoting conversion to sustainable economic and environmental development.

With such an environmental ethics, our right to intervene in a landscape is both bound and sanctioned by personal, community and global values. As landscape architects, we should be leaders in the formation and articulation of those values. Through our everyday work with public and private individuals and corporate, local, national and international clients we should be driving the environmental agenda forward. We should offer our skills, knowledge and energy in a *pro bono* capacity to the communities in which we live, in order to promote an environmental ethics to those we live among and the politicians who serve them. We should also, through our institutes and associations, work at a national and international level in persuading fellow professionals and governments of the efficacy of the environmental ethics.

In answer to the question of to what purpose do we intervene in a landscape, I argue for a paradigm of landscape architecture based on ecology, community and art (Plate 2). We intervene to promote sustainable

John Hopkins

development that integrates social, economic and environmental values in order that communities may live the good life; this requires that we express the human/nature relationship in a particular place through art. Are there limits to our interventions? The limits are ethical as defined by our ultimate end (the good life) and environmental as defined by our ultimate means (environmental capacity).

How are our interventions sanctioned? Sanction is through collaboration with fellow professionals, politicians and the communities within which we practise and through the mechanisms and instruments of planning law. The growth in urban design is recognition of the complexity and interdisciplinary nature of development and of the need for surveyors, architects, engineers, planners, ecologists and landscape architects to work together. We also need to introduce environmental economists, sociologists, artists and others into the process. The growth in consultation is also a recognition that the people who we are designing for, i.e. communities – 'the ultimate client' – have a real interest and contribution to make.

When do we intervene, and what is 'good' or 'bad'? Who decides? Ultimately, the decision must be community based. However, there are two aspects to this question. One is environmental, the other aesthetic. With regard to the environmental aspect, it is good if it is sustainable. With regard to aesthetics, I have argued for a notion of art that is based on ecological and community values, where the artist or landscape architect acts as interpreter of the *genius loci* or 'spirit of place'. Classical economics, as we have seen, promoted individualism, which in turn led to a view of the artist's role as one of *self*-expression rather than expression of collective identity and community values. In these terms, a landscape design is 'good' if it is a manifestation of the 'collective cultural, historical, and philosophical identity of a community'.[58] Always question the ethics of contemporary designs, always look beyond the merely visual and photogenic, to the ideas, the philosophy, the motive. What is clear is that fashion and style are superficial, and usually act against the longer-term interests of the community; timeless design does not.

What we can achieve as landscape architects is bound only by our personal and collective limitations. Our personal and collective moral authority and power will come from a fully fashioned environmental ethics supported by creativity, technical expertise, political awareness and eloquence. We have a critical vested interest in the creation of good places where we can dwell, and where we and many future generations may live the good life. For we are the music-makers, and we are the dreamers of dreams … we are the movers and shakers, of the world for ever, it seems.

Notes

1 T. Turner, *City as Landscape: A Post-postmodern View of Design and Planning*; E & FN Spon, London; 1996; p58.

2 D. W. Meinig, *The Beholding Eye*, in Meinig, ed., *The Interpretation of Ordinary Landscapes – Geographical Essays*; Oxford University Press, New York; 1979; pp34–47 passim.

3 A. Gore; *Earth in Balance: Forging a New Common Purpose*; Earthscan Publications, London; 2000; p297.

4 J. Hopkins; 'Landscape architecture: ecology, community, art'; in Birksted, Jan, ed., *Relating Architecture to Landscape*; E & FN Spon, London; 1999; pp205–7.

5 J. B. Jackson, quoted in D. W. Meinig, ed., *The Interpretation of Ordinary Landscapes: Geographical Essays*; Oxford University Press' New York; 1979; pp228–9.

6 J. B. Jackson, edited by Ervin H. Zube, *Landscapes, Selected Writings of J. B. Jackson*; University of Massachusetts Press, 1970; p9.

7 Ibid; p9.

8 J. Dewey, *Art as Experience*; Milton Balch, New York; 1934.

9 Ibid; p339.

10 Ibid; p9.

11 Ibid; p7.

12 Ibid; p192.

13 C. Steinitz; Letter to the Editor, *Landscape Architecture*, May 1981; p442.

14 R. Solomon; *Introducing Philosophy: a text with readings*; 3rd edition; Harcourt Brace Jovanovich, San Diego; 1985.

15 Ibid; p512.

16 Ibid; p523.

17 E. O. Wilson; *Consilience: The Unity of Knowledge*; Little, Brown & Company, London; 1999; p332.

18 S. Davidson; *Human Rights*; Open University Press, Buckingham and Philadelphia; 1993; p2.

19 J. F. Henahan, ed; *The Ascent of Man: Sources and Interpretation*; Little, Brown & Company, Boston and Toronto; 1975; p180.

20 Ibid; p5.

21 Ibid; p6.

22 Ibid; p11.

23 Ibid; p15.

24 M. A. Lutz, *Economics for the Common Good*; Routledge, London and New York; 1999; p236.

25 K. Annan; Foreword in Worldwatch Institute; *State of the World 2002: Progress Towards a Sustainable Society*; Earthscan, London; 2001.

26 Worldwatch Institute; *State of the World 2002: Progress Towards a Sustainable Society*; Earthscan, London; 2001.

27 J. Stiglitz; *Globalization and its Discontents*; Penguin Books, London; 2003.

28 Wilson; op cit; p324.

29 G. Tyler Miller, Jr; *Living in the Environment: An introduction to environmental science*; 4th edition; Wadsworth Publishing Company, Belmona, California; 1985; p30.

30 Hopkins, op cit; p205–27.

31 H. E. Daly; *Economics, Ecology, Ethics: essays towards a steady state economy*; WH Freeman, San Francisco; 1980; p11.

32 H. E. Daly and J. B. Cobb; *For the Common Good: redirecting the economy toward community, the environment, and a sustainable future*; Beacon Press, Boston; 1994; p165.

33 H. E. Daly; *Beyond Growth: the economics of sustainable development*; Beacon Press, Boston; 1996; p14.

34 Ibid; p13.

35 J. S. Dryzek; *The Politics of the Earth: environmental discourses*; Oxford University Press, Oxford; 1997.

36 H. E. Daly; 'The perils of free trade', *Scientific American*, November 1993; p52; quoted in M. A. Lutz, *Economics for the Common Good*; Routledge, London and New York; 1999; p224.

37 Daly and Cobb; op cit; p361 et seq.

38 J. Jopling; *London: pathways to the future, thinking differently*; Sustainable London Trust, London; 2000; p28.

39 Worldwatch Institute; *State of the World 2002: Progress Towards a Sustainable Society*; Earthscan, London: 2001

40 P. Hawken, A. Lovins and H. Lovins; *Natural Capitalism: the next industrial revolution*; Earthscan, London; 1999.

41 Ibid; p9.

42 Dryzek; op cit; p141.

43 Daly and Cobb; op cit; p174.

44 R. Hambleton; 'Future directions for urban government in Britain and America'; *Journal of Urban Affairs*; JAI Press Inc; 1990; reproduced in R. T. LeGates and F. Stout, eds, *The City Reader*; Routledge, London and New York; 1996; p297.

45 Dryzek; op cit.

46 Ibid; p3.

47 Ibid; p43.

48 Ibid; p15.

49 Ibid; p191.

50 Ibid; p197.

51 Ibid; p90.

52 Department of the Environment, Transport and the Regions; *A Better Quality of Life: A Strategy for Sustainable Development for the United Kingdom*; 1999; available from the Stationery Office.

53 R. Rogers et al; *Towards an Urban Renaissance: final report of the Urban Task Force*; Department of the Environment, Transport and the Regions; E. & F.N. Spon, London; 1999.

54 Office of the Deputy Prime Minister; *Living Places: Cleaner, Safer, Greener*; HMSO, London; 2002.

55 Ibid; p39.

56 N. Rao and K. Young; 'Revitalising local democracy', in R. Jowell et al (eds), *British Social Attitudes Report: the 16th report*; Ashgate, Aldershot;1999.

57 K. Worpole and L. Greenhalgh; *The Richness of Cities – Urban Policy in a New Landscape: final report*; Comedia & Demos, London; 1999; p19.

58 Hopkins; op cit; p207.

Part 2

The Design context

Chapter 3

Making places different

Alan Tate

Introduction

Landscape architecture involves conscious decisions to change external places for purposes of utility and beauty. This chapter argues that the achievement of utility with beauty is the product of a radical approach based on a clear understanding of the place to be changed. It argues that only with such an approach can landscape architecture make places different.

Geoffrey and Susan Jellicoe observed in 1975 that "the popular conception of landscape architecture has been that it is an art confined to private gardens and parks ... it was only in the present century that the collective landscape has emerged as a social necessity".[1] It might now be argued, however, that the period from the outbreak of the First World War in 1914 to the fall of the Berlin Wall in 1989 – the era of national socialism and communism in Europe – was the core period of the "collective landscape" and that we are returning to a period of greater private control of designed landscapes.[2]

Architecture professor Marc Treib noted more recently that "throughout history, landscape design has embodied and expressed the values of a culture: at times the power of the state, at times the aesthetics of those at a distance from power".[3] This observation is reinforced by comments from the

landscape architect and artist Martha Schwartz that "corporate bosses are our new kings and queens" and from Anne-Mie Devolder, director of Architecture International Rotterdam, that "contemporary garden design is now pursued in the service of companies wishing to see their corporate identity underscored by a beautifully conceived garden".[4]

      Schwartz and Devolder affirm that in the last twenty or so years the "collective landscape" has come increasingly under private control. This is demonstrated by the increasing number of books being published on the subject. Many of them, like Michael Sorkin's *Variations on a Theme Park: The New American City and the End of Public Space*, have abundantly self-explanatory titles. Most of them address trends towards private ownership and/or design and/or management of urban public space – and the outcomes of that trend.[5] A concurrent trend identified by cultural geographers is for people to "create their own city for themselves, a combination of the various places that are important for that individual".[6] This reflects landscape architect Peter Latz's comment that "nowadays everyone goes [to parks] alone; the dog owner, the diver, the cyclist. There is no such thing as a park for all."[7]

      Most accounts of the history and theory of landscape architecture tend to focus on the deeds of designers and on their words and on the words of professional critics. But landscape architects act, by and large, on the decisions

3.1
West Edmonton Mall, Edmonton, Alberta

and directions of individual clients or individual representatives of client bodies. They are paid for spending other people's money, and they follow instructions in order to ensure that they are paid themselves. Their work therefore expresses not only their own values but also the values of their clients. This leads to a situation characterized by the view that "you can't produce sensible design without a sensible client"[8] and where, in the worst cases, corporate and institutional clients "want something green, on the cheap and done yesterday".[9] Similarly, it has been argued that urban green space in The Netherlands suffers from "programmatic standardization ... spatial sameness ... compartmentalized planning ... low-grade maintenance ... and low levels of initial investment".[10] In short, form follows funding.

Levels of maintenance are a key issue in any review of the work of landscape architects. Schwartz has compared having a landscape to "deciding to have a child or a pet: if you don't have enough money to build or care for the project properly, then you shouldn't have it".[11] Landscape architect Michael van Valkenburgh has used a similar analogy: "the way people execute landscapes is comparable to getting a dog, putting it in the basement and going to look how it's doing two years later".[12] And in Europe, as in North America, "as landscape architects, we draw up plans according to fixed conditions and budget and planning constraints. Our work comes to an end the day we hand the project over to the client."[13]

This is not altogether new. Humphry Repton commented nearly 200 years earlier: "it is rather upon my opinions in writing, than on the partial and imperfect manner in which my plans have sometimes been executed, that I wish my Fame to be established".[14] This does, however, underline Hopkins' argument in Chapter 2 that it is critical to achieve the support of all relevant constituencies – particularly communities and their politicians – for the "collective landscape" to survive and thrive. All designed landscapes require unity of purpose and continuity of care for the conscious decisions from which they derive to remain explicit.

Values in landscape architecture

I have suggested that the fundamental purpose of landscape architecture is to change external spaces so that they provide utility with beauty. This is, of course, a simple definition that can be applied to all design disciplines. But it is probably more appropriate for landscape architecture than the Vitruvian objectives for architecture of providing "commodity, firmness and delight" – particularly because, as Leatherbarrow has pointed out, "these objectives pertain to buildings ... not to a discipline".[15] In the case of landscapes, commodity can be

3.2
Rousham,
Oxfordshire
(William Kent,
1685–1740): ha-ha

equated to utility, and delight (or the provision of pleasure) can be equated to beauty. Some landscape architects might argue that words like "durability", "sustainability", "integrity" or "authenticity" should be substituted for "firmness". They all represent important values. But I would suggest that these are secondary values that might dilute the clarity of creating places that provide utility with beauty.

Regrettably, Capability Brown (1716–83), author of the "beautiful" style in English landscape architecture (or landscape gardening as it was then known) left little written record of his design philosophy. Brown's admirer and successor, Humphry Repton (1752–1818), the leading exponent of the "picturesque" style, was more prolific. He concluded his *Defence of the Art* by arguing that "the perfection of Landscape Gardening consists in the fullest attention to these principles, *Utility*, *Proportion*, and *Unity* or harmony of parts to the whole".[16] This is, essentially, utility with beauty.

More recently Martha Schwartz has argued that "people inherently react to something beautiful" and "respond to the quality of space, the proportion of space, color, light, rhythm, texture".[17] She commented, at the same time, about (her fellow) Americans having a "narrow view … of what is essential to life. Functionality as a value reigns over beauty. We're a nation of low riders; we don't really value beauty and it shows".[18] Schwartz has attributed this pragmatic approach to everyday urban landscapes to what she calls "wilderness fantasy" – "allowing an incredible amount of ugliness to spread across the landscape … while imagining that we inhabit a beautiful wilderness". This is similar to John Brinkerhoff Jackson's observation that Americans "still revere the forest –

perhaps more than any other people, with the exception of the Canadians – as a place for recreation and rest and rich impressions".[19] Schwartz went on to identify a view that "since a shopping center isn't wilderness … it's okay to surround it with a parking lot with no trees".[20]

North America has a predominantly urbanized populace, which seems to enjoy the extraordinarily ambivalent belief that beauty belongs in art galleries and exurbia but that the principal role of everything in between is no more – nor less – than to function efficiently. By contrast, Christophe Girot has argued, from a European perspective, that "landscape is the historical result of the different uses made of a place, its climate and its topography. It is also the cradle of the history of the human species".[21] Girot went on to suggest that "the real field of action for a landscape architect is in the space between the two extremes of a chaotic, modern urban world, and a world of conserved nature. It is the landscape architect who … seeks an equilibrium, a quality of life and an individual identity for each place, even the most disadvantaged." Not remarkably different, then, from Schwartz's argument.

Girot also identified two of the most important values in landscape architecture: time and place (or context). Of time he wrote that "the work of the landscape architect is a long-term task, a humble and none too lucrative job which differs from that of the architect in terms of the time and the scale involved … rather than fossilizing the landscape and framing it in a single period, it is a matter of finding the link which unifies different times".[22] Similarly, Alain Provost, designer of the majority of the Parc André Citroen in Paris, which incorporates Gilles Clément's *Jardin en Mouvement*, asked the question "What garden is not 'in movement'?"[23] And in much the way that Girot wrote about "the link which unifies different times", Provost spoke about tradition being contemporary and suggested that "modernity lies in a tradition reviewed and corrected, in the cultural roots of everybody."[24]

The term *genius loci* (literally the genius – or spirit – of the place) was first used in connection with landscape architecture by the poet Alexander Pope (1688–1744) in his letter to the Earl of Burlington in 1731.[25] It is an enigmatic term that has "many shades of meaning" – including "abodes of special beings … energy fields … authenticity … narrative … local distinctiveness … essence … character … ecosystem … pantheism … panpsychism … and many more".[26] Despite these many shades of meaning and the ambiguity that they may cause, I reject the argument that *genius loci* "mystifies the design process and is damaging any attempts to construct places of meaning and significance".[27] Applied in its broadest sense *genius loci* recognizes the importance of context to the creation of places that provide utility and beauty. In much the way that members of the medical profession adopt a process of examination, diagnosis and prescription, landscape architects need first to understand

the places that they are involved in changing. They need to understand, at the very least, the social, economic, geological, ecological and climatic forces that determine their current status.

3.3
Parc André Citroen, Paris (Alain Provost et al.)

Although Capability Brown did not record his views on landscape architecture in writing, his biographer Dorothy Stroud reproduced excerpts from letters between him and the Reverend Thomas Dyer in 1775 in which both correspondents refer to Brown's ideas on "Gardening and Place-making".[28] And this may be the first reference to what has become – like "genius of the place", "sense of place" and simply "place" – a term that is now liberally and lavishly applied to most forms of environmental design.[29] Jackson noted, for instance, that "'Sense of place' is a much used expression, chiefly by architects but taken over by urban planners and interior decorators and the promoters of condominiums, so that now it means very little".[30] He suggested, however, that "a sense of place is something that we ourselves create in the course of time ... the result of habit or custom" whereas "others ... believe that a sense of place comes from our response to features which are *already* there".[31]

The landscape historian John Dixon Hunt has argued that "landscape architecture, locked into a false historiography, is unable to understand the principles of its own practice as an art of place-making".[32] Hunt described place-making as "fundamentally an art of milieu" that "involves not only inhabitants and users but the history of the place that is made or remade, the story of the site over time. Time and process lie at the very heart of landscape architecture …".[33] Hunt's recognition of the significance of time in landscape architecture, and that processes occur over time, is important. I would suggest, however, that the practitioner Provost's account of his approach to individual sites is more instructive: "we must distinguish between two types of site: those that have a body, have marrow, have a soul, a certain character, in which case it's better to be moderate, and those which have no special interest and where strong intervention is a virtue and not a fault for me – hence my own interventionism".[34]

The importance of understanding and interpreting a site before intervening in its human and biological processes is a fundamental value in landscape architecture. This was succinctly expressed by the professor of landscape architecture Barrie Greenbie in the mid-1980s when the American Institute of Architects was opposing licensure for landscape architects.[35] He described landscape architecture as "land + architecture … the composition of elements that nature provides, together with creations of human activity, in such a way that they serve human purposes without destructively violating natural laws and relationships".[36] Greenbie went on to distinguish between *landscape* architecture and *building* architecture as thinking "first of *what is there*, rather than what one can *put there*".

The social commentator Ken Worpole has also identified the importance of context as a generator of differentiation in a world where independence and individuality are becoming more highly valued: "mass production of landscape is no longer appropriate in a diverse and multi-cultural society, and issues of quality and context are now much more important".[37] Along with this validation of "quality and context" comes a recognition of the value of authenticity in the urban public realm. It has even been argued that "Americans now shop in malls that look like cities and in cities that look like malls".[38] The striking similarity of the now virtually ubiquitous shopping malls, strip developments, big-box stores and business parks is well documented. The architect and urban designer Michael Sorkin is particularly articulate about what he terms Cyburbia, the "ageographical city".[39] Sorkin has long pleaded for "a return to a more authentic urbanity, a city based on physical proximity and free movement and a sense that the city is our best expression of a desire for collectivity".[40] Cyburbia, it might be argued, is based on collective commercialism – and while its manifestations may be more overt in North America, they are no less insidious in the rest of the western(ized) world.

An ageographic world is anathema to a discipline whose limited theoretical base does at least include an exultation to "consult the genius of the place". This begs the question of how landscape architects can address a world in which "time has sped up and space has collapsed".[41] Landscape architects generally work on a site-by-site basis and are one small group of contributors to a massive tableau with a multitude of other contributors – from governments and corporations to individual landowners. Landscape architects since Frederick Law Olmsted (1822–1903) have had a continuing concern with larger-scale landscape planning issues as well as single-site issues. Indeed, the scale of work undertaken a century later by the landscape architect Ian McHarg (1920–2001) and his disciples was probably instrumental in the decline of the private garden as a vehicle for practice of the discipline. Indeed, it was only in the 1990s that garden design regained significance in the curriculum of professionally accredited programmes in landscape architecture.

There has also been increased engagement with the wider urban landscape – reflecting, in particular, the re-population of post-industrial cities. This has been formalized under the title "landscape urbanism", which is seen by some as a vehicle for addressing what has been termed "after sprawl".[42] Although "landscape urbanism" could be regarded as an oxymoron or simply a new label for large-scale urban design, it is now sufficiently well embedded in the environmental design lexicon for there to be academic programmes and professorships that adopt that title.[43]

There certainly should be recognition of the extent to which international standardization has been fuelled by an electronically driven global marketplace. Nevertheless, the Jellicoes, in their "Epilogue: Towards the Landscape of Humanism", concluded that the greatest threat to human existence "may not be commercialism, or war … or consumption of capital resources … but rather the blindness that follows sheer lack of appreciation and the consequent destruction of those values in history that together are symbolic of a single great idea".[44] Theirs was not the only epilogue to draw attention to humanism as a fundamental principle of the discipline. In his final editorial for *Landscape Journal* Kenneth Helphand called for the reassertion of "landscape architecture as a humanistic as well as pragmatic pursuit".[45]

Vociferous commentaries on urban sprawl notwithstanding, we should be aware that North America does not have a monopoly on inhumane landscape architecture. The external spaces of the French Bibliothèque Nationale, for example, are a striking example of obliviousness to context and to human comfort. Their principal components are a series of steep hardwood steps and a sunken courtyard. Girot asked of the courtyard, "What is a bit of pine wood from Les Landes doing in the middle of a library in Paris?"[46] In his novel *Austerlitz* W. G. Sebald gave a reader's perspective on the project, describing it as a "hideous, outsize building, the monumental dimensions of which were evidently inspired by the late President's wish to perpetuate his memory … in its outer appearance and inner constitution unwelcoming if not inimical to human beings … and runs counter to the requirements of any true reader".[47] He too

3.4
Bibliotheque
Nationale, Paris:
external steps

3.4
Bibliotheque
Nationale, Paris:
external steps

addressed the absurdity of introducing "about a hundred full-grown stone pines … transported, how I do not know, to this place of banishment". An ageographic antithesis of authenticity?

Girot, like Greenbie, has commented on the unhelpful divisions that continue to exist between the environmental design professions – particularly between *building* architects and landscape architects.[48] This has been described, in its most extreme form, as "modern architecture's repression of the landscape and its relegation of landscape architecture to an open space, a tabula rasa, a podium for a sculptural object".[49] This tendency to divorce buildings from their settings is one of the most regrettable aspects of a discipline that is ideologically (and literally) adjacent to landscape architecture. Schwartz has described this as a form of "territorial behaviour and egomania that is preventing architects from participating in holistic design".[50] The design educator Norman Potter argued that "education and design practice are too often handicapped by identity-fixations. The words by which people describe themselves – architect, graphic designer, interior designer, etc. – become curiously more important than the work they actually do".[51] Most landscape architects relish building-related work but despair of architects' frequent reluctance to conceive their work in a broader context. This is part of the "identity-fixation" to which Potter referred.

Potter offered a definition of design as "conversion of constraint into opportunity".[52] More recently it has been argued with respect to landscape architecture that "designing does not mean providing answers to fixed conditions, but should be a search for questions and how to answer them".[53] These definitions support the contention that landscape architecture is, first and foremost, a design discipline whose principal role is meeting human needs for utility with beauty in the external environment. They also suggest, in turn, that landscape architecture has always been, and should continue to be, a radical or essential activity – one that understands the forces that created a place and that takes account of its essence before seeking to change it.

Jane Amidon, in her book *Radical Landscapes*, talked about "capacity for radical thought" as a prerequisite for evolution. Amidon presented portraits of a number of recent high-profile landscape architecture projects as "radical landscapes" that demonstrate a "knitting of past to future with the present of the landscape".[54] Her assessment of what constitutes a radical landscape seems very sound. But her choice of late-20th-century examples seems to suggest that radicalism is a relatively recent phenomenon. It isn't. Appreciating the forces that shape places – their roots, their character, their essence, their use (what Provost called their body, marrow and soul) – before seeking to change them is the most fundamental and enduring value underpinning landscape architecture. Where Amidon might be right is in her suggestion that "content and effect" are currently valued more highly than "strictly formal concerns".

The second abiding value of landscape architecture is characterized by William Kent (1685–1748), who, in Horace Walpole's words, "leapt the garden fence and saw that all nature was a garden". The significance here is the first part of that statement: that the "whimsical, impulsive, unintellectual, in fact almost illiterate" Kent, "born in Bridlington of humble parents", looked at places in a fundamentally different way from his predecessors – and influenced others to do the same.[55] Kent, Brown and Repton, like Le Nôtre in France, were, of course, working primarily on private estates, whereas for most of the 20th century – the century in which landscape architecture formally became a profession in North America and Britain – has been an era of what the Jellicoes called "the collective landscape". The similarities of approach are, nevertheless, greater than the differences.

The third value that should be significant to landscape architects is the understanding of their own discipline's history. Even George Hargreaves, a globally pre-eminent practitioner and academic, has acknowledged that only in his 40s did he develop an "appreciation of landscape history and its importance to his practice".[56] Perhaps this is a repercussion of the modernist denial of the history of landscape architecture.[57] It also reflects the fact that it is only in the last quarter century that landscape architects in North America have been regularly addressing the remaking of post-industrial urban sites. A better sense of the history of the discipline would undoubtedly help practitioners to define their ongoing role.

Values applied

I will look here, in roughly chronological order, at statements and works by and about a number of prominent landscape architects. This is not intended to be even a summary history of landscape architecture and its practitioners. It is simply intended to give some evidence of what I have suggested are the timeless values of landscape architecture: understanding of a place and its context, a radical or essential approach to changing it, and an awareness of the temporal dimension of such changes.

Humphry Repton noted that Brown "observed that nature, distorted by labour and expence, had lost its power of pleasing with the loss of its novelty; and that every place was now become nearly alike. He saw that more variety might be introduced by copying nature, and by assisting her operations."[58] An early Sorkin? Turning to his own work, Repton commented that "all rational improvement of grounds is necessarily founded on a due attention to the CHARACTER and SITUATION of the place to be improved: the former teaches what is advisable, the latter what is possible to be done". Character, he suggested, is "wholly dependant on ART" whereas situation "always depends on NATURE, which can only be assisted, but cannot be entirely changed, or greatly controlled by ART".[59]

Frederick Law Olmsted, who was a journalist before he became a landscape architect, also wrote extensively about his work. He and Calvert Bowyer Vaux (1824–95), effectively the founders of the profession in North America, developed the "American Pastoral" urban park – "a reflection of the smooth-flowing lines of Brown's 'Beautiful' style and Repton's 'Picturesque' style ... a distinctly American response to the vast scale and rapid rectilinear growth" of New York.[60] Charles E. Beveridge, editor of the Olmsted Papers, noted that Olmsted "created a comprehensive body of theory about landscape design that was so original that few of his contemporaries grasped its full meaning. His emphasis on the psychological effects of scenery gave his design principles a firm base independent of the 'battle of styles'. Not aesthetic theory but the very health of the human organism became the touchstone of his art".[61] In much the same way that Repton commented about Brown's work being criticized because of its many imitators, so Olmsted's latter-day partner, Charles Eliot, suggested that Olmsted's work was original "in the sense that it was

3.5
Bow Bridge,
Central Park,
New York

reasoned, whereas most work in the same field merely follows the pattern of whatever happens to be considered the usual, fashionable, or proper thing ... his appeal was always to fundamental principles".[62]

It was this kind of fundamental approach that drove Olmsted's former colleague Horace William Shaler Cleveland (1814–1900), the under-

3.6
Lake, Central Park

3.7
Bryant Park,
New York: allée

acknowledged pioneer of landscape architecture in the American Midwest, to urge the Minneapolis Park Commissioners to purchase outlying land for public use ahead of the spread of the city. In his *Suggestions for a System of Parks and Parkways*, Cleveland implored the Commissioners, "If you have faith in the future greatness of your city, do not shrink from securing while you may such areas as will be adequate to the wants of such a city … look forward for a century, to the time when the city has a population of a million, and think what will be their wants … they will have wealth … but all their wealth cannot purchase a lost opportunity, or restore natural features of grandeur and beauty".[63] Cleveland's visionary approach – an early form of "landscape urbanism" – has given that city what has been justifiably described as "the best-located, best-financed, best-maintained public open space in America".[64]

Geoffrey Jellicoe (1900–96) described his Kennedy Memorial at Runnymede (Plate 3) as his "own adventure into a new field, of Allegory … the simplest of devices with which to captivate the mind".[65] Jellicoe cited Stourhead ("the outstanding eighteenth century example of allegory in land-scape"), John Bunyan's *Pilgrim's Progress* (where "the journey is one of life, death and spirit") and Giovanni Bellini's painting the *Allegory of the Progress of the Soul* (which "shows how pure geometry can create the sublime out of natural landscape") as precedents for the project.[66] Some people suggest that

3.8
Ira C. Keller
Fountain, Portland,
Oregon

there is a degree of post-rationalization in the way that Jellicoe spoke and wrote about his projects. Equally, Treib concluded his seminal piece "Must Land- scapes Mean?" with the suggestion that "significance is not a designer's construct that benignly accompanies the completion of construction … not the

3.9
Waterwall, Paley
Park, New York

3.10
Garden for VSB
headquarters,
Utrecht, The
Netherlands
(West 8)

product of the maker, but … [is] created by the receivers".[67] Unlike his (slightly younger) American contemporaries Garrett Eckbo, James Rose and Dan Kiley – to whom "the received body of historical landscape architecture was taken as meaningless because its significance belonged to other places and other times" – Jellicoe appears to have used his immense historical knowledge to drive his design work, even if it is more explicit in his written records than in the work itself.[68]

    The Ira C. Keller Fountain in downtown Portland, Oregon – designed by Angela Danadjieva (b. 1931) in the office of Lawrence Halprin and Associates – and Paley Park in midtown Manhattan – designed by Robert Zion (1921–2000) – were built shortly after the Runnymede Memorial and are both relatively small, re-made central sites. The fountain, completed in 1970, occupies a single block of 3,700 square metres; Paley Park, completed in 1967 and

3.11
Secret Garden for
BO01 event,
Malmö, Sweden,
2001 (West 8):
dreams of the sea
and imaginary
relationship with
the Swedish forest

completely rebuilt to the same design in 1999, occupies the 390 square metre former site of the Stork Club. Both projects were driven by strongly humanist intentions, and both are abstractions of the essential materials of landscape architecture – limited paving materials, a single species of tree and dramatic fountains. They remain landmarks in the history of landscape architecture, not least because they demonstrate that the discipline is most potent when it defies expectations rather than conforming to them.

Projects like these helped to establish the conditions for the work of two of the most publicized current practitioners – Martha Schwartz (Martha Schwartz Inc.), based in Cambridge, Massachusetts and Adriaan Geuze (West 8), based in Rotterdam (Plates 4 and 5). Many of their projects have been on a relatively small scale – including some that have been temporary installations rather than permanent schemes (for instance, their respective pieces for the BO01 housing exposition in Malmö, Sweden in 2001) – yet they are both engaged in critical practice relative to the emerging field of landscape urbanism. And both of them provoke reactions of the type "Oh my gosh, they're landscape architects and they do projects where they don't use plants?" from ostensibly aware critics.

Meyer suggested that Schwartz's work illuminates, first, that "landscape architects are engaged in a practice that is as enmeshed in the cultural as it is the natural, the artificial as much as the real"; second, "how blinded many landscape architects are to the pervasiveness of vernacular, suburban, and industrial landscapes, and how these shaped spaces may provide source material and inspiration"; and third, "the tendency to limit landscape architecture's scope to spaces worthy of the pursuit: urban parks, corporate headquarters and

3.12
Jailhouse Garden,
King County Prison
(Martha Schwartz
Inc.): ceramic
topiary and water
features

3.13
Federal Courthouse
Plaza, Minneapolis

plazas, fine gardens, campuses, and so on".[69] Some view her work as overt use of irony. Certainly it can "go against the grain" – particularly projects such as the re-making of Jacob Javits Plaza in lower Manhattan (Plate 6), which mocked city authorities for the rigidity of their requirements for traditional seating and

lighting units. But Schwartz's projects demonstrate levels of engagement in cultural and technical inquiry, and practical innovations and risks, that are exemplary in a profession whose creativity is its primary justification.

The extrinsic values of Adriaan Geuze and West 8 are comparable to those of Martha Schwartz. Geuze and West 8 also strive for "explicit integration of different disciplines and the bridging of extremes between small and big scale" while "ignoring the unwritten laws of traditional design attitudes, by crossing the boundaries of … professional fields".[70] Geuze is never shy about articulating the fact that his intrinsic values derive from his upbringing and education in The Netherlands – and not least the human-made qualities of that landscape. That background has given Geuze and his colleagues an approach to their work that is uninhibited by romanticism or unquestioning pragmatism. It is radical and realistic, and "sometimes even vulgar".[71] Their often-cited design for Schouwburgplein in central Rotterdam is praised for its programmatic flexibility, revered for its material diversity, and sometimes held suspect as a landscape without (woody) plants. Their recent proposal to replicate the white cliffs of Dover, the traditional first view of Britain on a channel ferry, at Jubilee Gardens, directly opposite Waterloo Station, London's European rail terminal, typifies their fine sense of irony.

Finally, it is worth exploring the values of two emerging landscape architects: Claude Cormier, who worked with Martha Schwartz before establishing his own practice in Montreal, and Vietnam-born Andrew Cao, now practising in Los Angeles and teaching at California State Polytechnic in Pomona. Two of Cormier's better-known projects – the Blue Stick Garden at the Jardin des Métis garden festival and Nature Légère (Lipstick Forest) – involve abstractions from nature, painted sticks representing a pixilated Himalayan poppy and

3.14
Schouwburgplein, Rotterdam

transformation of the structural columns of the Montreal Convention Centre into a swathe of pink tree trunks (Plates 7 and 8). Cormier noted that the Blue Stick Garden was driven by physical and cultural site specificity and that his practice is "active in shaping people's perceptions of the world around them instead of merely providing a service that caters to convention."[72]

Cao, winner of the Rome Prize in landscape architecture in 2002 from the American Academy in Rome, includes in the values to which he introduces students:

- don't be afraid to get in touch with your emotions – usually the first concept is the best
- visit the site and "connect" to it – consider the complete environment … not purely plants or particular materials
- learn from the past but do not imitate it
- take chances – but be prepared to step back and simplify
- be humble but opinionated
- take pride in whatever you do
- good manners and creative sensibility carry more weight than a glossy portfolio.[73]

Such values would be equally valuable to established practitioners.

Conclusion

This chapter is based on the view that landscape architecture involves the creation of external places for purposes of utility with beauty. It highlights the value of context (or *genius loci*) and radical approaches in the discipline and notes that, for radicalism to be fully effective, projects must be executed and maintained to meticulous standards. The chapter focuses on landmark figures in the history of the discipline and on latter-day iconoclasts. I would suggest, however, that many of those landmark figures were also iconoclasts in their own time. This suggests two things: first, that current practice should be viewed as an integral part of the ongoing story of the discipline; second, that radicalism – making places different – remains the essence of landscape architecture.

3.16
Nature Légère
(Lipstick Forest),
Montreal
Convention Center
(Claude Cormier)

Notes

1 Jellicoe, Geoffrey and Susan (1975) *The Landscape of Man*, Thames & Hudson, London, p. 7.

2 Lorzing, Han (2001), *The Nature of Landscape: A Personal Quest*, Rotterdam, 010 Publishers, p. 146.

3 Treib, Marc (2002) "City, Park, Rotterdam" in *The Public Garden: The Enclosure and Disclosure of the Public Garden*, Architecture International Rotterdam and NAi Publishers, Rotterdam, p. 151. This is comparable to the blurb on the 1987 softback North American edition of the Jellicoes' *The Landscape of Man*, which reads, "throughout history men [sic] have molded their environment to express or to symbolize ideas – power, order, comfort, harmony, pleasure, mystery ..."

4 Schwartz, Martha (May 2003) in a keynote address to "Landscapes on the Edge", Congress of the International Federation of Landscape Architects/Canadian Society of Landscape Architects in Calgary, Alberta; Devolder, Anne-Mie (2002) "Breeze of AIR: Innovative concepts for urban gardens in Rotterdam" in *The Public Garden*, op. cit., p. 10.

5 The outstanding example of this genre remains, of course, Jane Jacobs' *Death and Life of Great American Cities* (1961), but the level of output has expanded since the early 1990s with examples like Michael Sorkin's *Variations on a Theme Park: The New American City and the End of Public Space* (1992); Joel Garreau's *Edge City: Life on the New Frontier* (1992), James Kunstler's *Geography Of Nowhere: The Rise And Decline of America's Man-Made Landscape* (1994); Maarten Hajer and Arnold Reindorp's *In Search of New Public Domain* (2001); and *Sprawl and Public Space: Redressing the Mall*, from the US National Endowment for the Arts (2002).

6 Hajer, Maarten and Reindorp, Arnold (2001), *In Search of New Public Domain*, Rotterdam, NAi Publishers, p. 56. Similarly, Devolder, op. cit., has suggested that "public spaces in heterogeneous urban areas should provide city dwellers with the opportunity not just to meet but also to avoid one another" (p. 12).

7 Latz, Peter (April 1998), lecture at Harvard University.

8 This view was first put to me by Mark Way (subsequently managing director) of architects RMJM when we were working together on a project in Hong Kong in the 1980s.

9 Schwartz, Martha in Young, Pamela (July/August 2003) "[Urban] Jungle Warfare" in *Azure Magazine*, Markham, Ontario, pp. 62–7.

10 Luiten, Eric and de Jong, Frank de Josselin (2002), "Four Shades of Green" in *The Public Garden*, op. cit., pp. 44–9.

11 Schwartz, Martha (1997) in *Martha Schwartz: Transfiguration of the Commonplace*, Washington DC, Spacemaker Press, p. 107.

12 Van Valkenburgh, Michael (April 2003) in address to the "Large Parks – New Perspectives" conference at Graduate School of Design, Harvard University.

13 Brands, Bart and Loeff, Karel (September 2002), "Jenseits der Äasthetik: Beyond Aesthetics" in *Topos European Landscape Magazine*, no. 40, Munich, Georg D W Callwey, p. 61.

14 Repton, Humphry (1806), *An Enquiry into the Changes of Taste in Landscape Gardening to which are added, Some Observations on its Theory and Practice, including A Defence of the Art*, London, J. Taylor as republished (1969), Farnborough, England, Gregg International, p. 171.

15 Leatherbarrow, David (2001), "Architecture is its Own Discipline" in *The Discipline of Architecture* (edited by Piotrowski, Andrzej and Robinson, Julia Williams), Minneapolis, University of Minnesota Press, p. 85.

16 Repton (1806), op. cit., p. 174.

17 Schwartz (1997), op. cit., p. 110.

18 Schwartz (1997), op. cit., p. 108.

19 Jackson, John Brinkerhoff (1994), *A sense of place, a sense of time*, New Haven, Yale University Press, p. 85–6.

20 Schwartz, op. cit., p. 108.

21 Girot, F. Christophe (2000), "Towards a general theory of landscape" in *Rehacer paisajes: Architectura del Paisaje en Europa (Remaking Landscapes: Landscape Architecture in Europe) 1994–99*, Barcelona, Fundación Caja de Arquitectos, p. 87.

22 Girot (2000), ibid., p. 91.

23 Provost, Alain (2003) interviewed in "Contemporary French Landscape Architecture" in *Studies in The History of Gardens and Designed Landscapes*, London and New York, Taylor & Francis, p. 208.

24 Provost (2003), ibid., p. 204.

25 "He gains all points, who pleasingly confounds,/Surprizes, varies, and conceals the bounds. Consult the Genius of the place in all/That tells the Waters or to rise, or fall ..."

26 Brook, Isis (2000), "Can 'spirit of place' be a guide to ethical building?" in Fox, Warwick, *Ethics and the Built Environment*, London and New York, Routledge, pp. 139–51.

27 Moore, Kathryn (June 2003), "Genius loci: hidden truth or hidden agenda?" in *Landscape Design*, no. 321, Reigate, Surrey, Landscape Design Trust, pp. 44–9.

28 Stroud, Dorothy (1975), *Capability Brown*, London, Faber & Faber, pp. 156–7.

29 In much the way that there has been a rise in the number of books lamenting the "demise" of the city, there has been a synchronous rise in the number of books addressing "place" and "place-making", such as Tony Hiss's *The Experience of Place: A new way of looking at and dealing with our radically changing cities and countryside* (1990), Joseph Rykwert's *The Seduction of Place: The History and Future of the City* (2000) and even Charles C. Bohl's *Place Making* (2002).

30 Jackson (1994), op. cit., p. 157. Jackson went on to say that "'Sense of place' ... is an awkward and ambiguous modern translation of the Latin term *genius loci*. In classical times it meant not so much the place itself as the guardian divinity of that place."

31 Jackson (1994), op. cit., p. 151.

32 Hunt, John Dixon (2000), *Greater Perfections: the practice of garden theory*, London, Thames & Hudson, p. 207.

33 Hunt (2000), ibid., pp. 2–3.

34 Provost (2003), op. cit., p. 208.

35 The AIA eventually withdrew its opposition.

36 Greenbie, Barrie (May/June 1986), "Restoring the vision" in *Landscape Architecture*, Washington, DC, volume 76, no. 3, pp. 54–7.

37 Worpole, Ken (2001), "Urban Parks in Europe: topology and geometry, economics and aesthetics", in M. Treib, *The Public Garden*, op. cit., p. 156.

38 Crawford, Margaret (2002), "Suburban Life and Public Space" in *Sprawl and Public Space: Redressing the Mall*, US National Endowment for the Arts, p. 30.

39 In a piece titled "Welcome to Cyburbia" in *Quaderns d'arquitectura i urbanisme*, Barcelona, Collegi d'Arquitectes de Catalunya, no. 23, Sorkin talked about "huge shopping malls anchored by their national-chain department stores and surrounded by their swarms of cars; in hermetically sealed atrium hotels cloned from coast to coast; in uniform 'historical' gentrifications and festive markets ..." (p. 21). In the same publication the anthropologist Marc Augé suggested ("Non-places and Public Space") that the increasing number of similar looking transport structures ("train stations look like airports look like hyper markets, etc") is a reflection of "a new form of world organization, a planetary system which is seeking a style ..." (p. 15).

40 Sorkin, Michael (1992), introduction to *Variations on a Theme Park: The New American City and the End of Public Space*, New York, Hill & Wang, p. XV.

41 This phrase is from John Beardsley at the symposium "Contemporary Landscapes of Contemplation", at the University of Minnesota, Minneapolis, October 2002.

42 Lootsma, Bart (September 2002), "Biomorphe Intelligenz un Landschaftsurbanismus: Biomorphic intelligence and landscape urbanism" in *Topos European Landscape Magazine*, no. 40, Munich, Georg D W Callwey, pp. 10–25.

43 The Architectural Association of London, for one, offers a master's degree in landscape urbanism; the University of Illinois, Chicago, has a graduate "concentration" in the field and appoints a "Jens Jensen Visiting Critic in Landscape Urbanism", and the University of Toronto advertised a position in "the emerging field of Landscape Urbanism" in spring 2003.

44 Jellicoe, Geoffrey and Susan (1987), *The Landscape of Man* (revised edition), Thames & Hudson, New York, p. 391.

45 Helphand, Kenneth I. (2002), editor's introduction in *Landscape Journal*, Madison, University of Wisconsin Press, vol. 21, no. 2, p. vii.

46 Girot (2000), op. cit., p. 90.

47 Sebald, W. G. (2001), *Austerlitz*, Random House, New York and Toronto, pp. 275–81. Sebald wrote, in précis, that "you find yourself at the foot of a flight of steps which, made out of countless grooved hardwood boards … surrounds the whole complex … once you have climbed the steps, at least four dozen in number … you are standing on an esplanade which positively overwhelms the eye … you might think … that by some mistake you had found your way to the deck of the *Berengaria* or one of the other oceangoing giants … when I first stood on the promenade deck … it took me a little while to find the place where the visitor is carried down on a conveyor belt to what appears to be a basement storey … this downward journey, when you have just laboriously ascended to the plateau, struck me as an utter absurdity … that must have been devised … to instill a sense of insecurity and humiliation in the poor readers … the inner courtyard and the curious nature reserve cut, so to speak, from the surface of the promenade deck and sunk two or three stories deep, which has been planted with about a hundred full-grown stone pines from the Forêt de Bord transported, how I do not know, to this place of banishment … and several times … birds which had lost their way in the library forest flew into the mirror images of trees in the reading room windows, struck the glass with a dull thud, and fell lifeless to the ground … I thought at length about the way in which such unforeseen accidents, the fall of a single creature to its death when diverted from its natural path … relate to the Cartesian overall plan of the Bibliothèque Nationale … and came to the conclusion that … the all embracing and absolute perfection of the concept can in practice coincide … with its chronic dysfunction and constitutional instability."
48 This is very much the familiar complaint, as made by Greenbie (1986), op. cit.
49 Meyer, Elizabeth K. (1996), "Transfiguration of the Commonplace" in *Martha Schwartz: Transfiguration of the Commonplace*, Washington, DC, Spacemaker Press, p. 7.
50 Schwartz (2003), op. cit.
51 Potter, Norman (1969), *What is a designer: things.places.messages* (Fourth edition published 2002), London, Hyphen Press, p. 23.
52 Potter (1969), ibid., p. 23.
53 Brands and Loeff (2002), op. cit., p. 64.
54 Amidon, Jane (2001), *Radical Landscapes: Reinventing Outdoor Space*, New York, Thames & Hudson, pp. 7–9.
55 Fleming, John, Honour, Hugh and Pevsner, Nikolaus (1999), *The Penguin Dictionary of Architecture and Landscape Architecture*, 5th edition, pp. 316–7.
56 Hargreaves, George (April 2003), opening lecture to the "Large Parks – New Perspectives" conference at the Graduate School of Design, Harvard University.
57 See, for instance, Hunt, John Dixon in Treib, Marc (1993), *Modern Landscape Architecture: A Critical Review*, Cambridge, MA, MIT Press.
58 Repton (1806), op. cit., p. 6.
59 Repton (1806), op. cit., pp. 48–9.
60 Tate, Alan (2001), *Great City Parks*, London and New York, Spon Press, p. 123.
61 Beveridge, Charles E. and Rocheleau, Paul (1998), *Frederick Law Olmsted: Designing the American Landscape*, New York, Universe Publishing (revised edition of 1995 publication under same name), p. 30.
62 Beveridge and Rocheleau (1998), ibid., p. 40.
63 Cleveland, H. W. S. (June 1883), *Suggestions for a System of Parks and Parkways for the City of Minneapolis* in Wirth, Theodore (1945), *Minneapolis Park System 1883-1944: Retrospective Glimpses into the History of the Board of Park Commissioners of Minneapolis, Minnesota and the City's Park, Parkway and Playground System*. Minneapolis, Board of Park Commissioners, p. 29.
64 Garvin, Alexander (1996), *The American City: what works, what doesn't*, New York, McGraw Hill, p. 63.

65 Jellicoe, Geoffrey in Spens, Michael (1994), *The Complete Landscape Designs and Gardens of Geoffrey Jellicoe*, New York, Thames & Hudson, p. 92. The principal component of the project is a deliberately difficult winding woodland walk up a series of uneven steps comprising 60,000 small granite blocks – which Jellicoe likened to a line of pilgrims – eventually revealing an orthogonal setting for an engraved stone flanked by a thorn tree, symbolizing Kennedy's catholicism, and an American red oak, which would colour up on each anniversary of his slaying in November 1963.

66 Spens (1994), ibid., p. 92, and Jellicoe, Geoffrey (1983), *The Guelph Lectures on Landscape Design*, Guelph, Ontario, University of Guelph, p. 86.

67 Treib, Marc (1995), "Must Landscapes Mean? Approaches to Significance in Recent Landscape Architecture" in *Landscape Journal*, University of Wisconsin Press, Madison, WI, vol. 14, no. 1, p. 60.

68 Treib (1995), ibid., p. 48.

69 Meyer (1996), op. cit., p. 7.

70 "Engineer meets Poet – West 8", exhibition catalogue (1999), Berlin, Aedes, p. 3; Molinari, Luca (2000), *West 8*, Milan, Skira Architectural Library, p. 7.

71 Weilacher, Udo (1996). *Between Landscape Architecture and Land Art*, Basel and Boston, Birkhäuser, p. 230.

72 Cormier, Claude (2001), "Le Jardin des bâtons bleus/Blue Stick Garden" in *Landscapes/Paysages*, fall edition, Toronto, Southam Magazine Group, p. 18.

73 Hines, Susan (April 2003), "After the Glass Garden" in *Landscape Architecture*, Washington, DC, vol. 93, no. 4, pp. 104–7.

1

Landscapes of the mind:
natural areas and countryside
character areas created to
identify and communicate the
special character of the
English landscape, wildlife
and natural features

2

Seating at One Tree Hill,
Greenwich Park, London. The
lookout on the hill is set
within the finest example of a
Baroque landscape in
England and is in direct
contrast to it, clothing the
curvilinear hilltop. The timber
for the seats and benches is
windfall sweet chestnut (the
original avenue tree of the
1660s layout), the bricks
reclaimed London stock, the
inscription on the seat from a
poem about Elizabeth I ('fair
Eliza virgin Queen') enjoying
the prospect, published in the
London News, c.1770

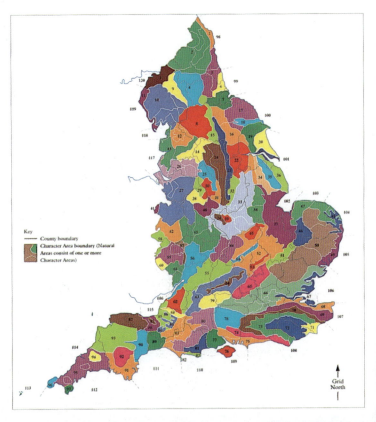

Key

— County boundary

Character Area boundary (Natural
Areas consist of one or more
Character Areas)

Grid
North

3 (opposite)
Runnymede Memorial to JFK
4
Garden for VSB Headquarters, Utrecht
5
Weeping Willow for BO01 event, Malmö, 2001

6 (opposite)
Jacob Javits Plaza, New York

7
Nature Légère (Lipstick Forest), Montreal

8
Blue Stick Garden, Métis sur Mer, Canada

9
Baltimore Inner Harbor, Baltimore, Maryland: plan for a competition
10
Coventry Urban Squares, England. 1: Broadgate Square

11
Coventry Urban Squares, England. 2: Council House Square
12
Crescent Eastbank Riverside Park, Portland, Oregon

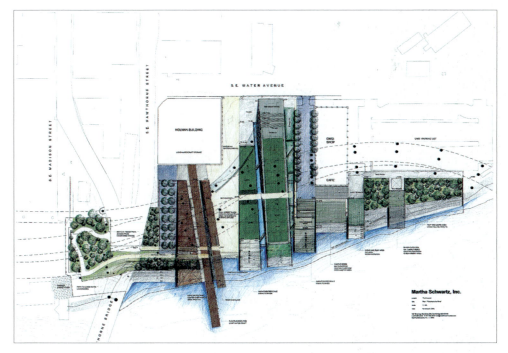

13 (above)
Doha Corniche,
Qatar: aerial view
of plan

14
Exchange Square,
Manchester,
England: industrial
artefacts were
included as
sculpture

15 (opposite)
HUD Plaza,
Washington, DC:
the objective was
to redesign an
inhospitable
exterior and create
hospitable spaces
for people

16
HUD Plaza: precast concrete edging provides seating around grass circles

17
Jacob Javits Plaza, New York City: snake-like double rows of continuous benches provide maximum seating for workers

18
Jacob Javits Plaza: green grass mounds break up the space for those seated

19
Mesa Arts and Entertainment Center, Mesa, Arizona: grand promenade with overlapping shadows from trees and architectural canopies creating a shady environment

20 (opposite, top)
Mesa Arts and Entertainment Center

21 (opposite, bottom)
Swiss Re Headquarters, Munich

22
Swiss Re Headquarters: planting reflects colours according to the season

23

Swiss Re Headquarters: use of colour is important for orientation

24

Le Parc de la Villette, Paris. The design by Bernard Tschumi Architects (1984) set a radically alternative and postmodernist manifesto for urban landscapes. It was seen to represent, in the words of Tschumi, 'one vast building, discontinuous but still a single structure overlapping in certain areas with the city and existing suburbs'

25

Vietnam Veterans Memorial, Washington, DC. Maya Ying Lin's memorial, dedicated in 1982 and located adjacent to the Washington Monument and the Lincoln Memorial, was designed to work with the landscape in which 'the object and the land are equal players'

26

Völklinger Hütte Iron Works in Saarland, Germany. Disused since 1986 and designated a UNESCO World Cultural Heritage Site in 1994, the monumental site is gradually being transformed, in part through the spontaneous growth of native vegetation, into a dramatic post-industrial landscape

27

The government's *Sustainable Communities Plan*, published in 2003, proposed a step change in housing supply in England. Central to its delivery in the Thames Gateway is *Greening the Gateway*, a policy document now underpinned by a series of strategic, multi-functional green or environmental infrastructure frameworks covering the whole of the Thames Gateway area and the eastern sub-region of London

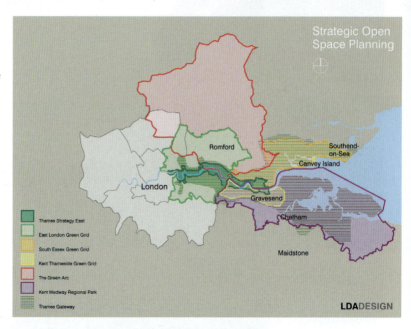

28

Thames Strategy East, prepared by LDA Design, provides a long-term spatial and planning policy framework to guide development in relation to the river from Tower Bridge to Gravesend. It promotes the protection and enhancement of existing natural, cultural and economic resources of value and the creation of new ones

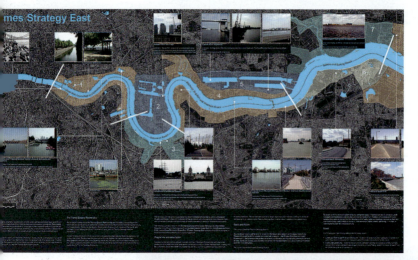

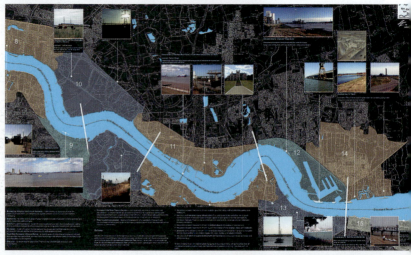

Chapter 4

Designer, client and user

Martha Schwartz

A landscape designer needs clients in order to function professionally, whether they be private individuals, corporate bodies, government departments or civic authorities. It is also necessary to be an articulate communicator in order to set up a constructive dialogue with the client and stimulate an interest in them for both the process and product of landscape design.

But to what extent can the designer control the process? There are limitations, since it is the client who usually sets up the process. They determine to what extent they wish to be involved or remain in control. You, the designer, have no real power in the situation. Your power is directly proportional to the desire your client has to have you involved. After all, it is not your money or resources that are being used; it's not your football.

However, a client is coming to you to transform the football into something else. If he has done his homework properly, he will know whether you are the type of designer that demands to have involvement (in terms of artistic control) or not, just by the type of work you have produced in the past, so it's a self-selecting process. For example, a developer who wants to do market-driven speculative houses is not going to show up at Frank Gehry's office expecting that he will be interested in doing this job. If, by mistake, he were to take this project to Gehry, the developer would start out with the

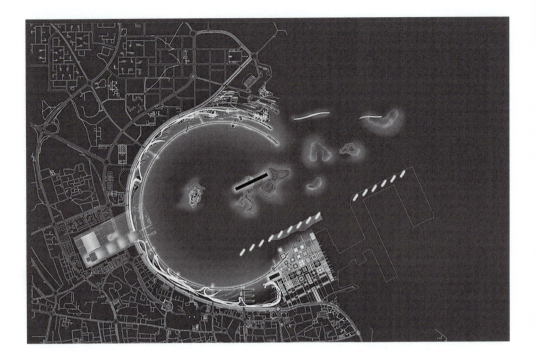

assumption that he will control the process, and this would certainly cause problems with the architect, since Gehry is a hands-off type of designer, who will tolerate only moderate intervention from the client. This is not to say that Gehry's clients have no control over the project, but if their objectives are in line with his, then the process will go more smoothly, with resulting satisfaction for all concerned.

Frank Gehry is a gifted artist; what he produces is moving and beautiful. He has also demonstrated the power and importance that an individual voice can have in building cities and that art, artistic expression and personal idiosyncrasy can be what is most treasured in a culture. I value this, because in the United States there is little recognition of the fact that art brings value. It is generally thought to be 'the cherry on top of the cake', a decorative and unnecessary gesture that simply embellishes. Europeans have a better grasp of how art functions within a culture, which is why Gehry got his first big break in Europe. The 'Bilbao effect' has illustrated how art, beauty and design can directly affect a city's economics and status in the world. I think that his artistry has educated the world to the potential of art to make a better world.

4.2
Doha Corniche:
computer
visualization

Public schemes

I have found that it is possible, however, to help your client to structure a working process and to help him or her gain confidence in the design process, thereby increasing the likelihood of success. This is especially important when a client has not had much experience of creating art/design while working within a public process. If you are lucky enough to be working with people who have had experience in administering public art and design projects, you are fortunate, since these people often have both ends of the spectrum clearly in their sights: they understand that the end game is to create a work of art that stands up to critical scrutiny and, at the same time, they can steer it through the entire process. The art administrator must protect the integrity of the artist or designer's work and still ensure that it conforms to standard best-practice criteria, while making sure that the public feels as though it has had an adequate say in the direction and even choice of the piece. However, most art administrators have not worked on large, expensive and complex problems such as are found within a public space project; and few public administrators, councillors or mayors have either the artistic ambition or knowledge about art, or artists, to know how to both direct and protect the artist while representing the needs of the community. It's a difficult balancing act.

4.3
Exchange Square,
Manchester: the
Hanging Ditch has
become a favourite
play place for
children

If it looks as though my clients have not been through such a process before, I have recounted other situations that have worked favourably in my experience and passed on the particulars of how these projects were structured. As it turns out, there is no standard practice for how to go about engaging in a public art/design process, and most municipalities are left to their own devices to try to figure it out. Some cities, such as Seattle, Washington, have extensive knowledge at the state, county and city level on how to structure and administer arts programmes. Seattle was one of the pioneers in implementing percent-for-arts requirements and spearheaded an important national movement. This is a programme that is funded by the federal government whereby one per cent of the budget for any government-funded project must be spent on art. Various states, cities and counties have also adopted this mandate. This is all predicated upon the desire of city leaders to go beyond minimum standards for building projects. Although more complicated, a well-structured process – from choosing an artist and/or designer, through the design stage to completion – presents the possibility for the creation of something of lasting cultural significance.

I consider Jacob Javits Plaza, the HUD Plaza (to some extent), the Mesa Performing Arts Center, and Exchange Square to be successfully run public projects. (See Plates 9 to 23 for illustrations of these and other projects relating to this chapter.) These all had well-thought-out processes. In all cases, a smaller committee was designated to represent a larger and diverse constituency. This group was empowered to make decisions. Milestones and deadlines were kept, and there were clear lines of responsibility vis-à-vis making certain that aesthetic decisions were kept within the purview of the designer. The committee made certain that practical, programmatic and money considerations were dealt with properly. It was always clear, in these cases, that *design excellence was a high priority*, and this was articulated often as a goal.

However, it is very true that while you work within the public realm, there are forces much greater than you that can have disastrous consequences. I have had projects that failed for the following reasons:

- After a two-year masterplan and public approval process, a mayor could not justify the expenditure of public money on public realm improvements (Baltimore Inner Harbor).
- The competition committee who chose us as the winning participant dropped out of the process, leaving us with an executive group that was

4.4
United States
Courthouse Plaza,
Minneapolis:
mounds are
designed so that
their sculptural
quality can be
appreciated even
in the heavy
winter snow

unenthusiastic about the winning design. Unfortunately, the city council members folded at the first sign of controversy and cancelled the project (Coventry).

- Political leadership changed mid-stream, and the project was too identified with the past administration (HUD Plaza).
- Insufficient public funding was put towards open space, compounded by the improper structuring of the team, resulting in the client (in this case the mayor of a major American city) not being able to have a direct relationship or contact with key designers. We, the landscape architects, were buried deep within the team, which was a turn-key project – that is, one where a developer manages the entire project, from partnering or procuring a contractor, designers, etc., and the client is presented with a completed project. It frees the client from the burden of project management and is often a way of guaranteeing the price but allows little transparency into the process. Unfortunately, it leaves both the landscape construction budget and the landscape architect buried within the architectural budget and hierarchy (Minneapolis).

A designer has to rely on his or her power of persuasion and ability to form relationships and to build trust with people. You can increase the likelihood of success and the adventurousness of the design if you can explain your ideas, illustrate where they come from and speak candidly about your process. In general, people do wish to understand what a design is 'about', and if you can provide a way for people to understand the ideas you are working with, they are grateful to feel included. An understanding of the ideas also helps to promote discussions, which furthers understanding, allows for dialogue, and builds relationships. It is important to remember that you are asking people to take a huge leap of faith with you, and that the uncomfortable position in which this places decision-makers must be respected. So, it is important that a certain amount of trust be built in order to make people feel secure enough, finally, to take the leap. Ultimately, a risk must be taken for anything new to be born into this world, and designers must seek out those decision-makers who also are risk-takers if they want to do adventurous work. The designer/artist must enable the client to take the risk.

Differing agendas

Should the landscape designer be forced to respond to other people's agendas? A designer can be forced to do anything. A designer must, however, set limits and define boundaries. I have been sent back to the drawing board many times to modify designs. I don't think that there is one project where I haven't compromised in some fashion. Sometimes these compromises have been to the detriment of the project; however, many times these changes have improved the project. I've learned that having to change a design is not necessarily a bad thing as long as the changes are done carefully so that the compromise is minimized and the integrity of the design is not damaged. This is why it is extremely important to have the designer involved in *all* the stages of a project, as changes happen continuously throughout the building process.

There have been situations where the changes or modifications were so demanding that the concept was too badly damaged to remain standing. Usually these modifications come during the 'discovery' portion of the design process. There is a time when both the designer and the client are learning about the site, and issues become apparent that were not there at the outset. Not only do you, the designer, come to more informed decisions as you go through the design process, the client does as well. During this learning curve, there may be many iterations and changes. It is typical that the initial fee

4.5
Swiss Re
Headquarters,
Munich: the design
recalls the
agricultural fields
that the building
has replaced

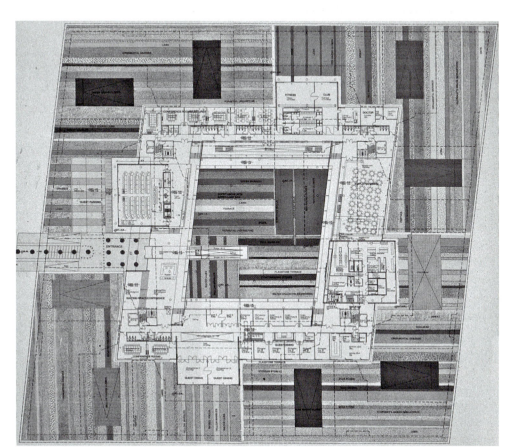

structure does not allow for this squishy process of discovery and must be revisited to enable the designers to keep up with the realities of the process.

There have been cases, such as Crescent Park in Portland, Oregon, where we had to re-design after going through an entire public design process, only to be told by the Environmental Protection Agency that the programme put forth by our client was not appropriate for this site. In this case, we had to start all over again, taking in these comments as a new starting point. This may run foul of timetables or even fees. We usually can work through these sorts of glitches, but we have also lost jobs over an inability to come to agreement over re-designs.

A designer has the choice to refuse projects that do not support his or her own objectives. However, there can be serious economic repercussions to being too selective. I was fortunate enough to be able to wait for the 'right' opportunities to come along. Even Frank Gehry struggled financially and emotionally for quite some time before he became recognized. There are many jobs that I would not take: namely, those with so much agenda that there is no room for artistic intervention. This is usually not related to how a site must function, but rather to the aspirations of the client. There is no project too small for us if the client's objectives are to create something that is unique, imageable and imaginative. For me, the most exciting projects are those where the client wishes to do something special. No matter how humble a project may be – it could be a highway on-ramp, a sewage treatment facility or a streetscape – any type of project could have an artistic agenda if the client held one. In this case, any type of project could be interesting.

Landscape designers – opportunists?

Landscape designers may see themselves as agents of mitigation and mediation, but are we really just opportunists? I can only answer this question for myself. Of all the things that I would describe myself as, it would not be as an 'agent of mitigation and mediation', certainly not without my green cape! I see myself as an artist and designer. That's what I can bring to a project; it's what I'm good at and what people ask me to do. They want my imagination. As we all know, people with good imaginations come in all shapes and sizes and with and without scruples. In art, it is crucial to have excellence and brilliance. Sometimes slip-ups in the scruples department can be weighted against a larger good (to wit, see *My Architect*, a film made by Louis Kahn's illegitimate son Nathan, about his famous architect father, that tried to bring into balance the gift that Kahn gave to the world versus the pain he brought to those who loved him).

None the less, there is the age-old question of whether a creative, generative person without scruples can be forgiven their lapses in scruples. I'm all on the side of forgiving such lapses if they result in general good for the world. We would probably not have a fraction of the art and culture we have if we were to eliminate artists who had scruple problems: Picasso, Toulouse-Lautrec, Jeff Koons, Edgar Allen Poe, Gauguin, Nietzsche, Roman Polanski, Andy Warhol, and so on.

Should landscape architects have more scruples than others? Landscape architects are no more holy than any other people and should neither place themselves nor be placed in a holier-than-thou position. Saying that, I believe that we should be operating in a way that helps the earth – and all who inhabit it – in any way we can, and to give something back so we leave this world a better place than when we entered it. But I believe this to be true for everyone. However, the topic of the environment is very wide and broad, and there are many, many ways to contribute to this topic, from the heroic site-specific art pieces done by the 'earthworks artists' of the 1960s (such as Robert Smithson, Nancy Holt, Michael Heizer and Walter De Maria), to ecological research, to devoting oneself to saving the snail-darter. These are all within the purview of 'landscape' and all make contributions. In a field as broad as landscape architecture, it is important that we must recognize that there are equally broad ways of making contributions, and that one way is not necessarily superior to another.

I am definitely an opportunist: I am always looking for opportunities to do something interesting. Given that the landscape is a much more complex, larger and more expensive canvas than most studio art, I must depend on others to supply my 'canvas'. This is, of course, part of a long tradition within the arts, where artists from Mozart, Beethoven and Michelangelo to Andy Warhol have needed patronage in order to make their art. Artists are probably the most voracious opportunists who have ever walked the earth, and I walk in those same well-worn tracks.

However, the charming thing about artists (although most artists are anything but charming) is that sometimes the world benefits immensely from the fruit of their opportunism. I'm not saying this happens every time or automatically, but the artists do make huge contributions to a culture, and ultimately through shaping that culture they become what it is remembered by.

The role of ethics

What role do professional, business and personal ethics, particularly in relation to the environment, play in boosting the quality of design? I think that it is not possible to proscribe the making of art or designing. There is no way to formulize it or to write a recipe for the creation of beauty. Although design with environmental sensitivity helps to achieve quality, it cannot achieve quality design without human inspiration and imagination. The creation of quality design has many aspects, and all design must serve the environment in a positive way – but this does not necessarily mean that the design will be inspired, memorable or beautiful. These attributes are needed to achieve the highest of quality. I think it is important that while building our environment we strive not to harm it and to do whatever is possible to work responsibly within it. However, by just respecting the environment, building conscientiously will not necessarily boost the quality of design. We must remember that humans are part of the environment, and that humans must make a cultural connection to a landscape, otherwise it will not be valued and maintained. The landscape must be designed in order to bring cultural relevance to a site. It is we who determine what happens upon our landscape, and if we design something that is interesting and attractive to us, than it will be used, embraced and maintained. If the design of the landscape invokes little interest or creates little value, then it will not be used or maintained and eventually will be lost. Ignoring design quality is not a sustainable strategy. *A landscape must make a connection to people if it is to be maintained and sustained.*

A landscape project is only partially done when it satisfies environmental issues, since people are part of the environment and determine the value of landscape. A design reaches significance only if it is embraced by people, and that includes sites that are left to natural process, national parks as well as highly designed, urban sites.

Responding to criticism

How should the landscape designer respond to comment and criticism? I think the answer to this question is: only to a certain degree. It is important to keep one's equilibrium when it comes to random opinions, or even overwhelmingly unified opinions from the masses. First of all, it is very difficult not to care what people say. All things being equal, I guess I would prefer it if everyone loved everything I did. This would certainly make life easier and more enjoyable for me: it would build more confidence. Given that I have had much criticism of my work throughout my career, I have had to learn to evaluate the criticism so that I can go forward without thinking of myself as a total crackpot or loser, try to learn from the criticism I felt to be valid, and not worry about the opinions that I thought were not constructive to my own growth.

Conversely, with the negative criticism comes positive adulation. I have always felt that if I embraced the positive feedback with the same amount of suspicion as the negative, that my own press would not carry me away. This is also a dangerous trap: not to believe that you're as good as a critic says you are.

Of course, there are a few people in one's life whose opinions are excruciatingly important. It's very difficult to expose yourself to these 'heroes' (such as the earthworks artists mentioned above), and the slightest criticism leads to intense pain and self-loathing. It's always better to sidle up carefully to these people if you want feedback. Smithson and the others invented a new language, a new art form that was the bellwether of the new environmental movement. It was non-commercial art (that supposedly couldn't be bought or sold through the effete New York gallery world) that was large, temporal, spatial, spare and strong and that created an awareness of the place. I wanted to create the same kind of art but related more to the built environment and the city.

I actually experience great pleasure if people like to be in the spaces I design. They are, after all, for these people as much as they are for me, and it is extremely rewarding when you can see that people like and are excited about these spaces. When a landscape turns out to be as good or better than you had imagined it to be *and* people love to be in it, it is a wonderful rush and tremendously satisfying.

I have examined the question of designer, client and end-user relationship, and satisfaction with landscape design through a series of questions, the answers to which reflect my personal experience. I shall finish by posing a further question: can we afford to ignore our audience? My answer: it depends on who our audience is!

Part 3

The benefits of the process
and its place in the wider
environmental agenda

Chapter 5

Who benefits from landscape architecture?

Catharine Ward Thompson

Whose landscape, whose culture?

Who benefits from landscape architecture? To move beyond the simple, aspirational answer – everyone – raises further questions. Who do we think the beneficiaries ought to be, and what is their place in the texture of society as a whole? Planning and designing our future landscapes takes place in a cultural context, and culture is not monolithic. So whose culture, whose landscapes, are we conserving, enhancing or developing anew? The challenge in these terms reflects the condition of the western world as we enter a new millennium. Do we properly recognise the value of cultural landscapes, should we make explicit the cultural assumptions implicit in the way we manage landscapes, and how do we weigh the importance of developing new cultural expressions against that of conserving the old? The European Landscape Convention, promulgated in 2000, lays emphasis on the contribution made by the landscape to the formation of local cultures, stating that it is "a basic component of the European natural and cultural heritage, contributing to human well-being and consolidation of the European identity". Yet recent approaches to heritage studies have highlighted the contested histories of places, recognising that there may be multiple views on the importance of a place's heritage and those who have contributed to it.

Parallel with this is the recognition that design for the future must be inclusive yet properly respectful of diversity, both in people and in places. This chapter explores the legacy of past attitudes towards landscape conservation and development in the context of Agenda 21, recent legislation and evolving theoretical approaches to urban society and rural landscapes. It uses this exploration to challenge notions of present beneficiaries and point to future beneficiaries of landscape architecture.

Changing rural landscapes and sustainability

In the 1970s, the UK government and its advisers, including ecologists, were still working on the assumption that the countryside was to be regarded as a resource for productive use rather than as an element of intrinsic value to be conserved for its natural or cultural features. Within all 'countryside' legislation there has been a section that emphasises the duty of those who implement it to have due regard for the requirements of forestry and agriculture. Implicit in this has been a prioritisation of the concerns of producers (landowners and managers). Yet, with pressure to reduce agricultural output, and with many marginal agricultural land uses in Britain becoming uneconomic, awareness has been increasing that the countryside is not just for farmers and foresters to do with as they like. Countryside access legislation in the 21st century reflects a desire for equality of access to the rural environment for an increasingly urbanised population. While 88 per cent of England is designated as countryside, only about 20 per cent of the population now lives there (although more than half claim they would like to do so, according to the Countryside Agency) and less than 2 per cent of the population is now directly engaged in agriculture or forestry. Only about 10 per cent of England's landscape is managed for conservation, amenity or public recreation purposes.

Today, many communities live an urban lifestyle in comparatively close proximity to the countryside but with no direct links to, or experience of, agriculture or forestry. Old mining communities are often cases in point. On the other hand, recent incomers and visitors to more remote rural settlements are likely to have a very different, and often more conservation-orientated, perception of life and the landscape than natives to the area, whose main concern may be unemployment and housing costs. The vociferousness of the 'countryside lobby' – protesting at Westminster on several occasions since 1999 against the UK government's perceived lack of concern over jobs, services and lifestyles, rather than presenting a unified set of values – no doubt masks a complex and multi-faceted view of the countryside coming from its landowners, workers and dwellers. How will these views be served by the legislative framework in a future where recreational and tourist agenda increasingly determine use of the countryside and demands on its image? There is a real challenge for landscape planning and community identity here. What is the cultural vision for a rural landscape when cultivation – the root of all culture, both literally and metaphorically – is a receding prospect?

Of course, the concept of 'countryside' is a cultural construct, just as those of 'wilderness', 'nature', 'scenic beauty' and indeed 'landscape' are, and perceptions and constructs change as society evolves. Rural communities have always been dynamic entities and not the stable source of unchanging values to which romantic visions and politics subscribe. The English enclosure movement, which reached its peak in the 18th and early 19th centuries, produced hedge and field patterns now seen as 'natural heritage' yet led to wholesale upheaval of rural economies and communities and was accursed by many, including the poet John Clare, at the time (Bromley 1990). In the Scottish context, much 'heritage landscape' is in fact an ecological wasteland that dates back in part to the agricultural clearances of the same era (Mackay 1995) but that still benefits from a picturesque attitude inherited from 18th-century aesthetic discourses. The Scottish landscapes of mountain, moorland and loch so often promoted in tourist brochures were described by Fraser Darling in the 1940s as a "wet desert". They are the result of systematic removal of those elements (deciduous forest, grazing cattle and, finally, the native population) that helped to maintain fertility, and then the steady expansion of sheep and deer, whose effects in excessive numbers (with associated muirburn – controlled burning of the heath moorland as grazing management) were generally to reduce the variety of species to a minimum and to impoverish already poor soil. This, as McVean and Lockie said (1969), is the "untouched wilderness", the "rugged grandeur" that is now being sold as a tourist attraction. Further, the Highland clearances, which had made way for sheep and deer grazing enterprises, were responsible for creating many of the crofting communities, where rural workers were resettled on marginally productive land, usually coastal, now also seen as cultural heritage. Heritage they certainly are, but from a period of contested histories and representing not a great, agriculturally sustainable tradition but one that was always marginal, fragile and, in many cases, enforced – a living scraped from poor soil, exposed landscapes and precarious land tenure.

Advances in ecological science and modern understandings of sustainability may mean that we now recognise the significance of interrelationships in geology, ecology, anthropogenic influences and rare scenic drama. They also demand that we are more explicit in recognising a heritage of over-exploitation (of both land and people) in landscapes that have been admired as beautiful for many centuries. The challenge in cultural landscape conservation

5.1
Crofting
landscapes on the
west coast of
Scotland: a cultural
landscape that has
always been
marginal

and development is precisely that it is a multi-dimensional issue. Concepts such as biodiversity conservation are more easily and simply encapsulated (hard though they may be to put into practice) than cultural diversity, which embraces anthropological, social, historical and archaeological interests, as well as those of agriculture, forestry, tourism and nature conservation. The combining of the Countryside Commission for Scotland and the Nature Conservancy Council to create Scottish Natural Heritage (SNH) in 1992 was one small attempt to unify approaches, but (as is apparent from its title) SNH has been predominantly a nature conservation organisation rather than one that focuses on cultural land-scapes. In England, the Countryside Agency was set up in 1999 from a merger of the Rural Development Commission and the Countryside Commission, with the aim of conserving and enhancing countryside while promoting employment and economic benefits for the rural population and access to recreation for all. Both SNH and the Countryside Agency have been engaged in developing guidelines on Landscape Character Assessment, which are an attempt to iden-tify and record some elements of the cultural landscape that make it distinctive at different scales, to support sustainable planning processes.

The United Nations Conference on Environment and Development (the 1992 Rio 'Earth Summit') helped define the principles of sustainability in the trio of economy, environment and equity but is perhaps best remembered for its 'Local Agenda 21' advice to public authorities, supporting the notion that global issues might best be tackled at a local level, taking into account cultural issues and the specificity of place. 'Environmental capital' has since been devel-oped as a concept that embraces environmental features or areas (such as

5.2
Dramatic scenery illustrates a heritage of over-exploitation of land and people

landscapes) and the environmental services or benefits that they provide (such as providing carbon sinks, or the location for a local cultural festival), in an integration that also attempts to recognise stakeholders in environmental enhancement. This accepts the fact that current cultural understandings alter the way we value landscapes and therefore how we plan and manage them.

It is only very recently in the UK that attempts have been made to create opportunities for all rural interests to participate in developing land management policies. In Scotland, the Highland Forum has been one example of an attempt to use non-statutory bodies to enable local participation. In the context of the developing pressure for national parks in Scotland (legislated for in 2000), the Cairngorms Partnership was set up in 1994, to draw together Scottish Natural Heritage, the Forestry Commission and local landowners, planning authorities and tourist interests to develop a common management strategy. In England, countryside and village design statements were developed to improve local design, respond better to local diversity and distinctiveness and provide a common and accessible design language to enable local people to participate in the planning process. Yet the emphasis has very often been on protecting and developing landscapes that are recognised as being of high quality, rather than working with communities in more mundane or degraded environments.

The Council of Europe's European Landscape Convention (2000) notes explicitly that the landscape is an important part of the quality of life for people everywhere: "in urban areas and in the countryside, in degraded areas as well as in areas of high quality, in areas recognised as being of outstanding beauty as well as everyday areas". It therefore sees the landscape as a key element of individual and social well-being as well as a component of cultural identity. It comments on the accelerating rate of change in the landscape, reflecting "developments in agriculture, forestry, industrial and mineral production techniques and in spatial planning, town planning, transport, infrastructure, tourism and recreation and, at a more general level, changes in the world economy". The convention promotes landscape protection, management and planning and points clearly to the need for public and community consultation and collaboration in developing landscape plans. It gives a perspective on the contribution the landscape makes to shaping people's lives and identities far beyond the economic value of its products. As of September 2004, Britain was not a signatory, yet the convention's emphasis on the importance of everyday landscapes, on the humble and mundane as well as the special, is one that still needs underlining in many areas of British policy, both public and private or non-governmental.

Celebrating cultural diversity and conserving humble landscapes

The historical view of landscape conservation in Britain, to take one theme from the European Landscape Convention, has tended to divide between that of the archaeologist and the design historian, with the latter traditionally focused on designed landscapes associated with historic buildings (or their remnants) and on the 'high art' of the social élite. While many people from all walks of life contributed to the classical canon of historic, designed landscapes in Britain, from those who dug lakes by hand to the travelling plant collectors whose trees now fill the arboreta, these landscapes represent only one strand of culture. Haynes (1983) has looked at rural landscape management and conservation from a different historical perspective. He has pointed out that the focus of protection from an archaeological point of view (as with designed landscapes) has been on sites and objects rather than areas, and this is too narrow a view. The importance of the broader landscape setting as a vital component of cultural heritage has been poorly served by current conservation legislation in both architectural and archaeological contexts, although this is an area of growing interest. The development of a professional specialism in landscape archaeology, which recognises the wider landscape, has much to contribute here.

There are further questions to ask about historic landscapes. The most complete of historic landscape patterns and associations, as revealed by archaeological relics and markings, are found in upland areas. This is not because the uplands were necessarily the most favoured landscapes for dwelling and cultivation but because they are the least disturbed landscapes in Britain. As with the crofting communities in Scotland, remnants of earlier cultural landscapes are very often remnants of marginal land-use patterns, rather than typical patterns of an era, because the most productive (and therefore most intensively used) will have been reworked and redeveloped most often in intervening years. For those interested in conserving cultural landscapes so as to celebrate cultural diversity, the challenge is to make the link between such a heritage of poverty and hardship and the heritage of grand and powerful landscapes promoted by a formalist approach to 'high' culture that held sway for much of the 20th century.

At one extreme are the designed landscapes of great country houses, valued as artistic enterprises and marketed so successfully by, for example, the National Trust; and at the other are rural, vernacular landscapes valued for their scenic beauty and designated as national parks (the Peak District, for example). The means for the conservation of the former are available in the range of protective legislation and grants available for restoration, whose authorisation is presided over by committees often chaired by the same class of powerful élite whose particular heritage is being protected. The administration of the UK Heritage Lottery Fund demonstrates just how much 'high' cultural assumptions (as Grandison (1999) has put it) still predominate as the basis of discourse in historical preservation. Yes, some lottery projects have focused more on community groups and local identities – Common Ground's visionary work on parish maps, for example, and the Local Heritage Initiative launched in 2000 – but we have yet fully to reconcile recent, and widely accepted, cultural theories with what they would mean in practice for our conventions with regard to landscape design conservation and designation. How do we link the celebrated grand landscapes of the 18th century with the history and heritage of those who were displaced to make way for them? We must take into consideration the many cultures and groups whose contribution to history and to our landscape and design heritage has not been well recorded or credited. In the context of the broader rural landscape, the use of special designations, such as national parks, for some landscapes still places too much emphasis on scenic attractiveness and too little on cultural and ecological processes, and implies that other landscapes are, by default, of lesser value. This does not sit easily with modern notions of cultural diversity and the importance of everyday places emphasised by the European Landscape Convention, nor with the "think global, act local" spirit of Agenda 21 (UN 1993).

Common Ground's use of the arts as a medium for encouraging communities to foster an interest in local environments is an attempt to heighten appreciation of the vernacular landscape and its associated

memories and cultural traditions, whether it be a local variety of plum, or a characteristic gate design, at a very local level and in fine-grained detail. These initiatives are an important step in beginning to value the humble and the everyday landscapes that are many people's heritage. Such laudable projects are perhaps easier to envisage in a rural context, where the 'culture' is reflected in physical form and the local population is limited, than in the urban context where most westerners now live. The recent revival of interest in allotments and smallholdings, which are all that is left of a cultural heritage that tied ordinary people to their local landscapes (as the landscape archaeologist Jaquetta Hawkes (1951) argued so passionately) until the bond was severed

5.3
The details that make for a distinctive landscape: a path and drystone wall take a diversion around an important field tree in the Peak District

by enclosures and clearances, has begun to be reflected in conservation and designation efforts (Crouch and Ward 1997). Unfortunately, such concern is, for the most part, at least 200 years too late. Cultural landscapes in towns and cities are often more complex to define. Although they, too, find expression in physical form, from private gardens and community plots to the town square and public park, the connection between physical form and current use is often much less direct, and there is far greater potential diversity and pace of change.

One of the challenges for those responsible for public open space is that treatment of cultural landscapes reflects broader issues of democracy. Corraliza's studies of Spanish urban spaces (2000) have highlighted the important and changing role that culture plays in our use of open space. He found that the non-spatial qualities of landscape (relating to emotional and personal issues such as motivation, age, etc.) are just as important as any spatial qualities, and that people (at least in Spain) preferred street environments where they can engage with other people (shops, cafés, shady boulevards) over parks or plazas. He has speculated that urban public parks are becoming places for *special categories* of people, such as children or old people, and the street is the *truly representative* public open space, the one that the whole population may feel comfortable in using. In Spain, as in many Mediterranean countries, there is a long tradition of promenading in the street – Barcelona's Ramblas is a prime such location – whereas in Britain, and perhaps in other more northern countries, the promenade has conventionally (since the 18th century at least) taken place in the royal or public park. Thus, Britain has had a tradition of the park as a place to 'see and be seen', which is perhaps matched by the street in other cultures. In an increasingly internationalised European society, we should be asking questions about this. Are British habits becoming more Mediterranean as we embrace the pavement café culture across Europe? And should open space planning in Britain be modified accordingly, or should it cling to distinctive ways of using space that need to be enhanced and reinforced? We have worried so much in recent years about the distinctiveness of our countryside landscapes and our buildings, but much less attention has yet been paid to culturally appropriate patterns of urban landscape design and use.

In a dense and increasingly urban society, public open spaces (and urban parks in particular, at least in Britain) are the places where democracy is worked out, quite literally, on the ground, and therefore the way such spaces are designed, managed and used demonstrates the realities of political rhetoric. Issues of ethnic and cultural diversity, and different perceptions of what is acceptable use, appropriate behaviour and desirable provision for access, must underlie decisions about landscape conservation, management and design.

The urban park as a cultural landscape

As author of the report of the British government's Urban Task Force, Rogers proposes that we "create beautiful places (in our towns and cities) that are socially cohesive, avoiding disparity of opportunity and promoting equity and social solidarity" (Rogers 1999: 47). In a densely populated and increasingly urban society, the outdoor environment sometimes offers the only places where people can come together – or at least share the same space – regardless of background, age, ethnicity or economic status. Inclusive access to high-quality landscapes and public open spaces is therefore a cornerstone of democracy and social equity.

The 19th-century park was designed, in the words of Frederick Law Olmsted, as "a kind of democracy, where the poor, the rich, the mechanic, the merchant and the man of letters, mingle on a footing of perfect equality" (Schuyler 1986: 65). The park was seen as a means to create a unified nation through a mutual appreciation of appropriate behaviour in a genteel setting. Today we need a more sophisticated understanding of the democratic process in order to identify, and provide for, the needs and desires of all in the diverse mosaic of our urban cultures. The political and public attitude towards a democratic, multicultural society changed, sometimes dramatically and painfully (witness the former Yugoslavia), as the 20th century drew to a close. The concept of a democratic society as a melting pot where cultural differences become homogenised within an overriding expression of national culture has largely been replaced with a more pluralistic ideal. Rather than expecting conformity, we now strive to accept diversity in needs, attitudes and expression, and therefore in provisions for society (Ward Thompson 1998), but can urban parks really satisfy such diversity? In a call for research on social relations and social interactions within public space in 2003, the Joseph Rowntree Foundation asked to what extent public spaces can really be seen as shared places and what benefits such shared places offer.

Such questions must be asked of parks that were originally designed for a single, predominant culture and raise the challenge of how adaptable historic parks in our towns and cities are. How much does their design, as opposed to their programmed use, need to change in the 21st century? The tension between determination by managers to restrict what is seen as inappropriate behaviour in a park and the desires of many users for more varied recreational opportunities has remained a constant from the 19th century to today. In the New York of F. L. Olmsted's time horse-racing in Central Park was controversial, and today it is immigrants wanting to play cricket in Prospect Park that is seen as dangerous or inappropriate. Different social and cultural groups have different perceptions of what is acceptable or safe behaviour, depending on traditions that may transcend class, race or ethnicity but that still reflect radically contrasting expectations of what is the 'norm'. Recreational sporting traditions may clash with other groups' expectations of large crowds and loud music to celebrate a holiday. Some conflicts can be resolved by time-programming rather than space-programming, but it is clear that only a truly participatory planning process will resolve them. The development of methods to identify potential stakeholders in an inclusive way, and to involve stakeholders effectively, is discussed later on in this chapter. Suffice it to say here that the level of sophistication and sensitivity of such methods must match, and even challenge, our evolving sense of what democracy can and should mean in practice in a multicultural landscape.

Yet, however sophisticated our planning processes are, certain time-less constants are likely to remain. Surveys of urban park use, e.g. by Comedia and Demos (1995), repeatedly indicate that the majority of users want to come by foot and will only do so on a regular basis if the park is within 3 to 5 minutes' walk of their home or workplace. The people who have most need for access to local public parks and the opportunity for sociability in a safe outdoor setting will always be those with least access (through age, economic status or infirmity) to private transport – children, the elderly, the unemployed – and so there will always be a demand for good access to appropriate, local open spaces.

Landscape as a restorative environment and a place to be oneself

A number of studies have claimed that being out in the landscape, whether in a city park, a town square or a countryside setting, is good for people's health. Beyond being a place for sporting and recreational pursuits, which may be good for physical fitness, the landscape is believed to play a vital role as a place where people get away from stress, relate to natural seasons and elements and experi-ence physical and psychological well-being as a result. There is increasingly strong evidence (e.g. Kaplan and Kaplan 1989; Ulrich et al. 1991) that access to some form of 'nature' is a vitally important part of access to open space and that the failure to provide such natural relief from the urban environment will have substantial health costs in the long run. The Kaplans (1989: 182) discuss the idea of the "restorative environment" in very much the same language that Olmsted used in the 19th century: "The struggle to pay attention in cluttered and confusing environments (such as crowded urban ones) turns out to be central to what is experienced as mental fatigue." The natural environment seems to have some special relationship to each of the four factors identified by the Kaplans as important to a restorative environment: being away from the source of the fatigue; being in a place that gives a sense of extent (even if just in the mind); fascination; and compatibility between one's inclination and environmental circumstances. In addition, say the Kaplans, the natural environment has an aesthetic advantage, since such settings are uniformly preferred over many other environments.

The idea that there is a minimum size of landscape unit necessary to get an 'interior' in which to escape into a restorative environment finds expression today in the ecological principles of Forman (1996), who uses the term 'patch size' to promote the concept of a minimum spatial volume necessary to provide a sufficient habitat for any particular species or community. Access to nature is determined by the proximity of such places as well as their size and shape, and Forman's concepts of patches, corridors and mosaics should also be helpful in thinking about open space networks for human needs; too often these concepts are applied to every species except *Homo sapiens*.

Public parks have been described as places for the meeting of strangers, but in a busy urban context is the public park the one place where people can actually be private, lost in the anonymity of the crowd or in a deeper and richer open space? In his study of parks and park users in the UK for the *Park Life* report (1995), Ken Worpole commented: "Many people said that they visited the public park for privacy now often unavailable in the media-dominated home" (Warpole 2000: 20). Such a visit allowed for an intimate personal space or time, "a way of regaining an interior world". Worpole goes on to describe the kind of space he believes people want: "A wooded, undulating terrain seems more conducive to human spell-making and intimacy than a world of hard surfaces – although there is much evidence that we can also find forms of intimacy and belonging in the urban crowd, in the public square or on the outdoor café terrace" (p. 22). Although Worpole believes that the modern city needs both wooded parks and urban squares, he has highlighted Marc Augé's observation (1995) that in the controlled spaces of modern urban commerce and design – shopping malls, airports, even some high streets – there is an automatic assumption of guilt about anybody not engaged in purposeful consumer behaviour. By contrast, he says, the free world of the public park has always evoked a pre-lapsarian world of innocence and autonomy.

As I have commented in my own study of American parks (Ward Thompson 1998), the symbolism of the park as refuge or paradise is deeply embedded in our psyche, a kind of cultural memory, and thus crimes that take place in parks assume a shock value out of all proportion to their frequency or in comparison to the likelihood of such crimes on adjacent streets. Perhaps subconsciously, we cling to the idea that the park should be a place of freedom and non-threatening nature, yet for many a park can also be a place of fear and anxiety. Burgess (1995) has demonstrated how women and people from ethnic minorities may feel excluded from wooded and secluded parkland landscapes because they worry about being attacked or getting lost. Older people also worry about accidents that might leave them injured and far from help (Ward Thompson et al. 2002). Yet the group most often blamed for unacceptable behaviour in parks – teenagers – have been shown to suffer themselves from considerable anxiety about using public open space, and young men are, in practice, most at risk from attack. Such anxieties, justified or irrational though they may be, have implications for younger children too. While children may enjoy the freedom that a natural environment offers for play and manipulation of their environment (in making dens, for example – their own 'private' worlds (see Titman 1994)), the very qualities that make for this freedom can also be perceived as dangerous, threatening or, at the very least, unsettling.

So we have here an intriguing pair of apparent contradictions. Firstly, the park or square as a public place for the meeting of strangers is also a place where people can be intimate, anonymous and therefore private. Secondly, the qualities of wooded parkland are desired because of their natural, intimate and manipulable qualities and yet are also feared because of this element of freedom and wilderness, which implies lack of control.

It is probably precisely the tension between these polarities that creates what is pleasurable in thinking about and using open space, and this has parallels with the Kaplans' (1989) concepts of coherence and complexity, legibility and mystery in the psychology of landscape preferences. It seems we need access to nature and its restorative qualities, but nature also provides very real challenges for us, both psychological and physical. The landscape may allow us to be more 'ourselves' but also tests the limits of what we can comfortably tolerate or confront. There is real enjoyment to be had in testing our physical stamina in outdoor recreation and in taking certain kinds of risks, and this may be lost if every environment becomes too safe; but equally there are many in our society for whom access to attractive outdoor environments is far too much of a challenge.

Access to the landscape

In the western world, at least, we have a demographic trend towards an ageing population, and there are increasing demands for elderly and disabled people, as well as people with certain kinds of health problems, to be more fully integrated into society. In Britain, approximately 16 per cent of the population is disabled, young or old, and many of these people have restricted mobility (Rogers et al. 1999). Despite recent legislation to require removal of barriers to access, there are still real difficulties in providing better access for all to high-quality open spaces throughout the urban fabric and into the rural landscape. For many disabled people, large parts of the urban open-space structure, including some pedestrianised streets and squares, are still hard to access, as is most of the countryside.

When the English and Welsh national parks' legislation was established 50 years ago, the challenge was to create a planning framework for conservation and to provide appropriate facilities for recreation. The success of these parks has been qualified by the realisation, expressed in the 'Rural White Paper' that country pursuits are currently largely the preserve of "the white, middle-aged, middle-class and able-bodied" (Department of the Environment, Transport and the Regions 2000a). For the new national parks being developed in Scotland (legislated for in 2000), and for the UK countryside as a whole, the challenge now is to provide a new model for the 21st century that allows the least restrictive access for all while conserving and enhancing the distinctive landscape character of each place. The experience of the foot and mouth disease epidemic in Britain in 2001, which allowed farmers to place temporary restrictions on all access through fields, gave many people a taste of the frustration that 16 per cent or more of the population face all the time in not being able to use footpaths in the countryside.

Despite initiatives in many parts of the world, progress towards improved rural access has been slow and difficult. In the US, the Americans with Disabilities Act (1990) has contributed to improved access through a compliance-based approach to provision, although this has also led to a standardising of details and materials that may be deemed counter to the notion of *genius loci*. In the UK, the 1995 Disability Discrimination Act laid down standards and guidelines but required each case to be determined on its own merits, allowing, at least in principle, the possibility for good, site-specific design solutions to be developed. The duty under the act to remove barriers to access (enforced in 2004) is a focus of attention for landscape planners, designers and managers of both town and countryside tourist attractions and recreational facilities. The Countryside and Rights of Way (CROW) Act (2000) in England and Wales required local authorities to prepare rights-of-way improvement plans to meet the "present and likely future needs of the public" and, in particular, to address "the accessibility of local rights of way to blind or partially sighted persons and others with mobility problems". There was a stated commitment to achieving a 10 per cent improvement in defining, maintaining and publicising the rights-of-way network by 2005. National targets for paths agreed with local authorities set an aim for 95 per cent compliance with three requirements – easy to find, easy to follow, easy to use – yet a survey in 2000 showed considerable local variation in the condition of paths, and many regions appeared to be far from meeting such a target (De Lurio 2002).

The Countryside Agency publication *Sense and Accessibility* states that two of the biggest barriers facing people with disabilities are poor-quality information and physical difficulty of access (Alison Chapman Consultancy 2000). Often, information does not provide enough detail to encourage or enable potential users; prior to the Fieldfare Trust's work with BT Countryside For All, there were no national information guidelines on access for all and few for improved access in rural settings. The most limiting physical barriers are structures such as stiles and gates. Permanent barriers, such as stumps and padlocked gates, are often installed (particularly along waterways) to prevent misuse of footpaths by motorcyclists, but they also make routes difficult or impossible to use by others, such as those with wheelchairs or prams (Inland Waterways Amenity Advisory Council 2001). The Countryside Agency has drafted good practice guidances for improving access to the wider countryside, which range from development of policy through to the implementation of physical improvements on the ground and the provision of information for prospective visitors. It proposes applying the principle of 'least restrictive access' to all practical works that take place in the countryside.

However, the equity of access to which the government's Rural White Paper makes commitment is a multi-dimensional issue. The white paper explicitly includes exploring how to encourage more people with disabilities, more people from ethnic minorities, more people from the inner cities, and more young people to visit the countryside and participate in country activities. Implicit in this is the notion that visiting or accessing the countryside for plea-sure can contribute to social inclusion, yet research has shown that there is a lack of adequate post-hoc evaluation to assess the benefits of countryside enjoyment and the effectiveness of projects to increase participation by under-represented groups (OPENspace 2003). A range of barriers to countryside enjoyment has been identified, from the financial costs incurred and lack of accessible transport to lack of appropriate activities to attract excluded groups and provide a positive and relevant experience. Many people lack confidence in visiting the countryside and have negative perceptions of it: they don't feel welcome, don't know where to go, worry about getting lost and feel uncomfort-able with the traditional image of regular users and groups.

In Scotland, the Land Reform Act (2003) and accompanying Scot-tish Outdoor Access Code enacted equivalent legislation to that for England and Wales, reflecting a similar desire for equity of access to the outdoor environ-ment at a time when Scotland's first national parks are being developed. The draft Scottish Outdoor Access Code continues a long-standing British theme whereby countryside users are allowed "responsible access", but it is assumed that they will follow certain norms of behaviour, however unfamiliar these may be to people who have grown up in inner cities and to those from different

ethnic backgrounds. Thus, although site design, management and maintenance will all have a significant impact on the participation of under-represented groups in countryside enjoyment, it is important to recognise the range
of cultural, emotional and psychological barriers to participation experienced by
such groups. The government in Britain is committed to supporting improvements in parks, both town and country, through lottery funding, Countryside
Agency grant schemes, etc. and sees community forests as a prime way of
creating accessible countryside for both urban and rural dwellers. Whether
such commitment and supporting legislation deliver good and appropriate
access, and whether such access contributes to social inclusion in practice,
remains to be seen.

As has been discussed earlier, the broader political and economic
landscape of the European countryside is one where reliance on agriculture as a
primary source of income is in decline and diversification of income source a
necessity. The recreational and tourist market is a vital part of the economy of
rural landscapes, and this creates some tension between the struggle to maintain agricultural output and the requirement to provide for appropriate access to
the countryside. As the tourist market increasingly includes visitors with some
mobility or sensory disability, including the growing percentage of the population aged over 65, high-quality design solutions that provide for inclusive
access will be the key to increasing any share of the tourist market. This applies
equally to town and countryside, and to provision for home and overseas tour-
ists. The challenge is to develop appropriate access provision and to design
details in a context where conservation of cultural landscapes and enhancement of local landscape character are also a priority, as highlighted by the European Landscape Convention. It is important that the wild or rugged nature of
some landscapes is not compromised, nor that the vernacular details of walled
field enclosure or stone paving, which are particular to a locality, are ignored or
obliterated. The concept of a 'recreation opportunity spectrum' (Driver 1990)
has been developed to link recreation activities, landscape settings and experiences and can provide an approach to access where provision is determined on
the basis of what is appropriate to visitors' reasonable expectations. It offers one
basis for linking landscape perception studies and effective, GIS-based information systems to good, inclusive landscape design.

On the urban scene, the establishment of CABE Space in 2003, part
of the Commission for Architecture and the Built Environment in England,
follows decades of neglect of urban parks and open space, as highlighted by
the government's Urban Green Spaces Task Force. The task force, established
in 2001, found that the majority of local authorities did not have any form of
parks or public space strategy, nor were they intending to implement one. One
of the many challenges now facing urban authorities is to develop and promote

high-quality urban spaces that are accessible to all. Work by Burgess (1995) and others (Ward Thompson et al. 2002) has pointed up how important it is to pay attention to the needs of women, ethnic minorities and vulnerable groups, including children, older people, and those with disabilities, in all aspects of landscape design and planning. This must inform broader issues of stakeholder involvement: identifying potential stakeholders whose voices might not be heard at present.

Stakeholder involvement

In the context of greater efforts throughout the western world to involve stakeholders in the political decision-making process, the challenge for landscape architects and planners is to find appropriate methodologies for engaging people, understanding their perceptions and responding to them. Participatory planning has been mentioned earlier as an important tool in designing and managing public parks and urban open space. In many rural areas, the landscape is at a critical point where its economic future is not assured and the consequences of change, economically, visually and socially, are potentially enormous, both for local inhabitants and for society as a whole. In such rural contexts, most of the local inhabitants will be either those whose livelihoods are directly or indirectly linked to the broader landscape or, increasingly, those who have deliberately chosen to live in a rural landscape because of its existing qualities. It is often only at the point when significant change is proposed in their environment that people want to get involved in the planning process and to make their opinions known. This may be a time when passions are aroused and the landscape is argued over most forcefully. But are landscape professionals as effective as they could be in helping people envision change and articulate responses to that change? What methods are appropriate to use? Are stakeholders readily able to engage in decision-making and the planning process, and are they eager and willing to do so?

The work of Kaplan, et al. (1998) and others reinforces the fact that landscape specialists have developed different perceptions from those of the non-specialist public, and it is important to engage and inform the latter directly in discussions about what landscape change might be like, and how acceptable it might be. Preference for a place is about more than just the visual: people bring previous experiences, expectations and their personal objectives to any evaluation they make of a place (Scott and Canter 1997), and therefore a person's background will help shape their perceptions. In a similar way, response to change will be informed by cultural and personal experiences and ambitions. Even relatively new initiatives, such as *Landscape Character*

Assessment (Countryside Agency and Scottish Natural Heritage 2002), which include criteria to do with developmental pressures and the direction of change in the landscape, have yet to engage adequately with stakeholders in what this change means to them.

Recent work on place evaluation (Scott Myers and Ward Thompson 2003; Scott 1998; Donald 1994, drawing on Canter (1977); and Kelly (1955)) confirms that, for local people, the role of the physical environment is largely to provide the setting for a social environment. Indeed, within the discipline of environmental psychology it is generally accepted that, while the physical environment has a significant role to play in everyday life, this role is rarely explicit unless a feature of the physical environment obstructs, prevents or otherwise interferes with a person's objectives. The relationship between the physical and social environments is transactional. In essence, if changes are made to the physical environment, whether people think that these are good or bad changes will depend on the extent to which the changes affect how people can carry out their jobs and tasks or take part in desired activities. Equally, if people's jobs or responsibilities change, what they want to do will also change, and so will their perception of the suitability of the physical environment. Furthermore, landscapes associated with memories of key emotional events can become part of people's personal identity. Changes to that landscape may trigger an intense and emotional response and can lead to strong reactions of hostility or grief.

Provision for effective stakeholder involvement in the planning process thus continues to be a challenge for those responsible. As a profession, landscape architects are involved very much with the visual and physical landscape but, in order to engage stakeholders meaningfully in decisions about change, it is necessary to employ methods that explore beyond these dimensions. A likely benefit of developing information technology will be systems that enable ordinary citizens to contribute their desires and visions for the future to a planning database linked to three-dimensional, GIS-based visualisations (Bishop and Gimblett 2000, Wherrett 2001) which are readily understandable and accessible. If such modelling systems can allow people to record their own important memories and desires and to engage with the emotional and social experience of landscape options, and not simply their visual implications, then we shall have a tool that really helps tap into what matters to people about the landscapes around them. At present, access to computer-based media, and the level of confidence with which people engage with such media, still exclude some categories of society, but this is likely to change very rapidly and there is a real chance of developing that ideal of participatory planning that Patrick Geddes promoted nearly a century ago.

Landscape of the electronic and the information age

What does communication and information technology mean for landscapes and their users? Many people have predicted negative effects, both for individual activities and for urban life as a whole, as modern telecommunications and information technologies mean that our community is increasingly a virtual one. Face-to-face contact with other people, it has been suggested, will have less and less to do with work, with social engagement and entertainment or with shared experience, as people undertake work, manage their lives and relax via the internet, the telephone and television. In Britain, up to 80 per cent of newly formed households over the next 20 years are expected to be single-person households (Rogers et al. 1999). We are thus looking forward to an urban society where more people are living in relative proximity than ever before, but where the regular daily social contact that comes from sharing homes or living close to one's workplace no longer pertains. It is an intriguing, if not disturbing, prospect – a physically close-knit society of strangers whose social group(s) may be dispersed across the globe.

Yet there is evidence that, although information technology does allow for greater flexibility in terms of location, particularly for some office functions, it is also resulting in new urban concentrations for face-to-face activity. People still seem to need human contact, and towns and cities are the place for that, even if technology allows us to do otherwise if we choose. Our friendships may be based on personal history and shared interests, regardless of the geography of individuals, and we may have regular contact with friends who live thousands of miles away, but we can also easily communicate with large numbers of local contacts. The internet has allowed groups to plan and organise events and to use open space much more readily than ever before. Whether it's an international demonstration in Seattle involving tens of thousands of people, or simply an informal game of football in the local park among friends, e-mail, websites and the mobile telephone allow such use of public open space to be organised very quickly, with very low overhead costs, and increasingly effectively. Today's teenagers are already masters of spontaneous socialising, relying on their ability to contact friends anywhere at short notice and on the prevalence of the café culture to provide places to meet without having to spend a great deal.

So, although the electronic revolution means we no longer need to go into the streets of our towns and cities to find out the news or to arrange to meet people and organise events, it does mean that we can now use those streets, squares and parks with much greater confidence that we'll find what we want there, meet whom we want, be able to do what we choose. Given that we are social animals, and that we crave real contact with each other and with nature, perhaps public open space will be more, and not less, used in future than it has been in recent decades. It also bodes well for inclusive access, where better information about what can be expected in any particular landscape should help disabled people, for example, to plan outdoor activities with some assurance that their aims will not be frustrated in practice. The work of CABE Space and other promoters of high-quality environments in the public realm will need to embrace imaginative uses of new technology to take advantage of the many opportunities potentially available in the design and use of open space. There will certainly be opportunities to explore what 'intelligent' landscape design (as opposed to building design) might deliver. Perhaps truly responsive landscapes will include opportunities for seating or ramps to rise up from or disappear into the paving, as and when we need it. Responsive information screens or surfaces will help us navigate unknown places, as well as, perhaps, giving us up-to-the minute data on aspects of the local microclimate or wildlife. Developments in the creation of virtual environments will lead to an intriguing, parallel world of virtual, 4-D space and time; perhaps in this context the value of engagement with the *real* environment will become more precious. There is no doubt that new technologies will allow us to enjoy open space in ways that are particularly well suited to our personal preferences and to the current trend towards individual expression, despite the fact that urban society and its demands are becoming increasingly diverse as a whole.

If we choose to look beyond our cities and towns, we shall certainly have access to more information than ever before about our countryside, but how much will we actually understand about it? It seems likely that, as

5.4
The experience of growing food and engagement with the natural world – important for children and for adults

5.5
Allotments can
reflect old land
uses and celebrate
new ones:
allotments in the
grounds of an art
gallery, Edinburgh

agriculture becomes ever more intensified in Europe, the countryside will be divided into areas of industrial-scale agriculture, which most people will never visit; areas of cultural landscapes, conserved as historic parks of some sort; and areas of 'wilderness' where people will go for active recreation and solitary or isolated experience. The last two categories are certain to be popular, but there will be ever-diminishing contact with the land as a productive resource unless it happens at a smaller and more personal scale. Philanthropists and those inter- ested in child development, from Goethe, Steiner and Geddes onwards, have insisted on the importance of allowing children to experience growing plants

and making the connection between plants and the food they eat (Macdonald 1992). In an urbanised society with an industrialised agriculture, this becomes harder than ever to achieve unless allotments or school gardens are accorded a key place in the structure of urban open space. Indeed, some people argue that the intensification of urban densities that is advocated by many urban designers, including Rogers, is not necessarily the best model for sustainable living and that the provision of personalised garden or allotment spaces within the urban fabric is what people want and need, for both psychological and practical well-being.

5.6
Garden shed in the grounds of an art gallery, Edinburgh

Many arguments have been produced for the value of community gardens or allotments in cities and a recent revival in enthusiasm for them. Francis (1987) sees them as a socially desirable provision that engages certain groups in the use of public open space who would not otherwise use a park. There is also evidence that certain immigrant groups find the ability to grow familiar plants and vegetables an important link with the experience they may have left behind, perhaps in a rather different cultural context. Such people may indeed see it as an economic necessity to grow some of their own food, a fact we often forget when we are acculturated to a society of fast-food and supermarket convenience. Whether or not the entire urban fabric should be modelled around personal or community allotment spaces, there is a strong case for some flexibility within the urban structure to allow for such uses or for other, perhaps less conventional, activities to arise and to wax or wane as the social fabric changes.

Precise plans, fuzzy frameworks and loose-fit landscapes

Looking to the future, it seems clear that new technology will be harnessed to satisfy old and unchanging needs, but also that new patterns of open space networks are being conceptualised that reflect new scientific and cultural understandings. We need precise plans to define artistic visions, function-specific space and the neat, safe and attractive parks that offer equity of access for all. But these plans may need to be within the 'fuzzy' framework of an open space network that is dynamic in aesthetic and ecological status, allowing for a larger mosaic, a patchwork of changing, loose-fit landscapes.

Kim Dovey (2000), Leanne Rivlin (2000) and others have explored 'loose-fit environments'; these are often undesigned, unregulated, left over, abandoned or ruined spaces that allow for a proliferation of activities and may serve a wide range of people's needs in ways that designed spaces do not. Such 'found' spaces can give opportunities for privacy in anonymity, as has been mentioned earlier, but perhaps especially offer a place for the marginalised in our society: age groups or social or ethnic groups not welcome in conventional, well-supervised parks. They may be conveniently located and offer a sense of freedom, but also of safety, for some who are poorly tolerated under normal conventions.

Phenomenological approaches to space typology, such as those explored by Dovey (2000), explore the difference between rooted, fixed, constrained spaces and those that are slippery, unconstrained, nomadic or migrant (the 'striated' versus the 'smooth'). Approaches to the former have focused on visual order, whereas the latter are associated with the haptic – the sense of touch. Most interesting is the concept of these loose, migrant spaces and what qualities make for such places of freedom and escape. Dovey associates them with the process of 'becoming', with a liminal, edge condition, one that shifts in quality and in space. Loose spaces, he says, aren't necessarily places with no rules but places where we're continually inventing new rules. For example, each time children start playing a game, they set up a place with their own rules, which may be tightly constraining but invented anew by them that day.

The key is how spaces are *used* and designed to be used; therefore the illusion that open, empty space is not constrained is incorrect – Beijing's Tiananmen Square may look very open, but its use is strictly constrained. Dovey suggests that Rem Koolhaas and Bernard Tschumi have got it wrong in Schouwburgplein and La Villette, for similar reasons: the emphasis on static, visual qualities of space do not in fact make for loose and free use of space, but a space where use is highly controlled and limited. Freedom is always risky; in slippery, loose places we need to be haptically involved to negotiate our way safely in space. None the less, the need for places of rich experience and for risk, not just for adults but for children and for childhood reminiscences, is particularly important. Work on children's perceptions of their environments has shown that loose-fit places can often provide important places of escape, especially for people with troubled childhoods. Roger Hart's seminal work (1979) has shown that children like to find and 'make' places for themselves that are quite different from those identified by adults. Yet the personal autonomy of children has been dramatically reduced over the last 20 years, even for those with secure backgrounds (Ward Thompson et al. 2002), and such opportunities for freedom may be rare. There are few supervised adventure playgrounds in

5.7
A loose-fit place where children can make up their own rules

Britain, school playgrounds (despite the work of Learning through Landscapes, Grounds for Learning, etc) continue to be very restrictive, and public playgrounds provide only for a narrow range of risk and experiment. We need to know more about how children understand potential risks and hazards and how to allow for unstructured and challenging play in the outdoor environment in ways that parents and teachers are prepared to accept (and that health and safety legislation can sensibly cope with), so that the pleasure of freedom can be enjoyed.

Baines (1999) has argued for the recognition of value in the waste lots, the derelict gap sites awaiting redevelopment but currently not managed, where opportunist weeds spring up and a sense of the uncontrolled makes for an air of excitement. For pre-adolescents, this may be the one place where it is acceptable (or at least tolerated) for them to break sticks and branches, to learn about the physical properties of things by testing them to destruction; for adolescents it may be the one place where they can 'hang out' without being under the disapproving eye of authority. The real countryside offers rich opportunities for such interaction with the natural environment – an interaction perhaps necessary for our full human development, but one that is considered vandalism or antisocial behaviour in any formal park and therefore denied legitimacy. It is likely that loose, semi-wild or derelict spaces – perhaps very small ones, not necessarily the extensive 'wild' spaces of urban ecological networks but places much more indeterminate, local and often shifting in location – are part of the answer. We need to re-evaluate, and perhaps re-value, loose-fit landscapes in society and in our designs on the land. If the concept of *genius loci* is about revealing the qualities inherent in a landscape, not putting things into a site in an attempt to import a predetermined quality from elsewhere, then maybe loose-fit landscape design can, for example, focus on reuse of found objects on site. Such landscapes might begin to reflect the diversity of urban culture and the specificity of place in a way appropriate to the value of individuals in our shifting society.

Who pays and what are the benefits?

In the context of asking who benefits from landscapes and landscape architecture, we must also ask who pays. If open access to the countryside is the ideal, who funds the surfacing of path networks, the maintenance of gates, etc.? These are issues that test commitment to and responsibility for inclusive access. The costs of managing open space in the public realm also create great challenges for urban authorities and test some of the details of democratic funding provision. In looking for creative solutions to the cost of managing urban parks, much has been made of the North American experience, where 'Friends of the Park' groups have taken on fundraising, management and other support activities. But there may be problems here too, despite the laudable engagement of 'stakeholders' in their local parks. Different interest groups may have different agenda, and such groups can become 'proprietors' in a way that may exclude others, marginalising those without the additional time or money to contribute. A dedicated local area tax base to fund urban park management is another theme being explored internationally, but such schemes also bring with them a danger of exacerbating socio-economic inequalities if they are applied at too local a scale, the wealthy areas ending up with better-maintained parks than the poorer ones. Such questions of funding for landscape management have, at their root, a much more fundamental challenge: does society believe that the quality of the outdoor environment really matters?

Ideas of sustainability and social equity have recently been combined with notions of environmental quality to produce the concept of 'environmental justice', first developed by the African-American community in the USA and defined by the country's Environmental Protection Agency in 1994 as the "fair treatment for people of all races, cultures, and incomes, regarding the development of environmental laws, regulations, and policies". Internationally, concern that minority and low-income populations bear a disproportionate amount of adverse environmental effects has led to a call for balanced and equitable access to good-quality environments for all. This has been taken up by UK politicians in the 21st century, particularly by the Scottish Executive, focusing attention on the need to improve life for those living in polluted or degraded environments. The demands of environmental justice require contributions from many areas of expertise and a recognition of international and local dimensions, as Rio's Agenda 21 reminds us. Yet surely landscape architecture has an important role to play here.

Landscape architects in many parts of the world express frustration at the lack of recognition for their work, for the valuable contribution they can make to people's lives. The problem, I suspect, is not that landscape architects are not appreciated, nor even that their designs are not good or striking enough, but that, despite current notions of environmental justice and quality of life, society at large has failed to recognise (or be persuaded) that landscape itself, and engagement with it, is vitally important to our well-being. If we believe that the physical, perceptual, cultural landscape is vital and that its quality affects our health as much as the food and water it produces (that production we now so rarely see or participate in) and the building ground it provides for our urban forms and constructions, then do we behave as if we believe it?

In England in 1971, 80 per cent of 7- and 8-year-old children made the journey to school unaccompanied by an adult; by 1990 this figure had fallen to a bare 9 per cent. Parents fearful for their children's safety on the roads have imposed more rigorous restrictions on activities such as cycling, walking and street play (Hillman et al. 1990). What does this mean for the development of our children? What hope is there for their environmental awareness, let alone urban sustainability and quality of life, in such a scenario? There are now attempts in some urban areas to check, if not reverse, such trends, but the challenges reflect broader issues to do with childhood development and the environments to which children have access. Children are able to articulate what they want, and it is also clear (Titman 1994, Ward Thompson 1995) that they view the landscape context they are given as a reflection of how society views and values them as people: do we give this enough weight in designing our everyday environments? There is empirical evidence of the importance to people of landscapes that include elements of 'nature'. There is a growing body of research on the kind of landscapes children like for play. And there is much circumstantial evidence that people want high-quality landscapes in which to live and work, and that they benefit from them in all kinds of ways, psychological, physical and practical. But there is very little empirical research demonstrating unequivocally that good landscape design is better than bad (or no) landscape design for people, or that ignoring the quality of landscape carries the risk of a health hazard. Perhaps it is too complex an issue ever to demonstrate unequivocally (why else do we allow so many children to spend their school playtime in such 'desert' playgrounds?), but that is a challenge for researchers within the profession. Whatever the evidence, most people, whether government funders or the person in the street, don't behave as if it were demonstrably the case that clear health benefits will emerge from good landscape design and conservation, and that there are enormous health risks associated with ignoring access to 'nature'. Until we make this link effectively, until and if we can get society (and particularly public funders) to recognise that good landscape design will, eventually, save hospital bills and that bad landscape design (or failure to give due weight to landscape quality) is too high a financial and health risk to justify, the true value of landscape architecture as a profession is unlikely to be recognised.

Landscape architecture is about process, about change, whether managing the slowly evolving change of biological systems or the rapid change of development intervention. Some change can be precisely predicted and planned for; some is characterised by the level of indeterminacy and imprecision necessarily involved. This is a metaphor that can equally be applied to society, and planning for society. If landscape architecture is to benefit society it must also help society understand the value of its open space and the complexity of the ecology in which humans participate: this shifting, changing environment essential to our lives and with so much potential to be life-enhancing, to be fun, to bring delight. In our increasingly urban society, public open space and publicly accessible landscapes are places to celebrate culture and cultural diversity, to engage with natural processes and to conserve memories. The way that people benefit from the landscape around them, and the inclusiveness of that benefit, will always serve a central function in society's self-definition.

Bibliography

Alison Chapman Consultancy, 2000. *Sense and Accessibility: how to improve access on countryside paths, routes and trails for people with mobility impairments*. Wetherby: Countryside Agency Publications.

Augé, M., 1995. *Non-places: introduction to the anthropology of supermodernity* (transl. John Howe). London and New York: Verso.

Baines, C., 1999. 'Background on Urban Open Space'. *Scottish Urban Open Space Conference*. Dundee: Scottish Natural Heritage and Dundee City Council.

Bishop, I. D., and Gimblett, H. R., 2000. 'Management of recreational areas: GIS, autonomous agents, and virtual reality'. *Environment and Planning B: Planning Design* 27, 423–35.

Bromley, P., 1990. *Countryside Management*. London: E & FN Spon.

Burgess, J., 1995. *Growing in Confidence: understanding people's perceptions of urban fringe woodlands*, Countryside Commission Technical Report, Northampton.

Canter, D., 1977. *The Psychology of Place*. London: Architectural Press.

Comedia and Demos, 1995. *Park Life: urban parks and social renewal*. Comedia and Demos: London.

Corraliza, J.-A., 2000. 'Landscape and social identity: the construction of territorial identity'. In G. Moser, E. Pol, Y. Bernard, M. Bonnes, J.-A. Corraliza and V. Giuliani (eds), *Proceedings of the 16th Conference of the International Association of People–Environment Studies, 'Metropolis: which perspectives? Cities, social life and sustainable development'*, Paris: Laboratoire de Psychologie Environnementale, Université René Descartes – Paris V.

Council of Europe, 2000. *European Landscape Convention*. Florence, 20 October 2000, www.coe.int/t/e/Cultural_Co-operation/Environment/Landscape/

Countryside Agency, 1998. *Barriers to Enjoying the Countryside*, Research Notes issue CCRN 11, November 1998.

Countryside Agency, 2002. *The State of the Countryside 2002*. Wetherby: Countryside Agency Publications.

Countryside Agency and Scottish Natural Heritage, 2002. *Landscape Character Assessment: guidance for England and Scotland*. Wetherby: Countryside Agency Publications and Edinburgh: Scottish Natural Heritage.

Crouch, D., and Ward, C., 1997. *The Allotment: its landscape and culture*. Nottingham: Five Leaves Publications (originally published in 1988 by Faber & Faber).

De Lurio, J., 2002. *Recreation – an Overview: environmental facts and figures*. The Environment Agency (www.environment-agency.gov.uk).

Department of the Environment, Transport and the Regions, 2000a. *Our Countryside: the future – a fair deal for rural England* (the 'Rural White Paper'). (Available at www.defra.gov.uk/rural/ruralwp/whitepaper/default.htm)

Department of the Environment, Transport and the Regions, 2000b. *Our Towns and Cities: the future, delivering an urban renaissance*.

Donald, I., 1994, 'Management and change in office environments', *Journal of Environmental Psychology* 14, 21–30.

Dovey, K., 2000. 'Spaces of becoming'. In G. Moser, E. Pol, Y. Bernard, M. Bonnes, J.-A. Corraliza and V. Giuliani (eds), *Proceedings of the 16th Conference of the International Association of People–Environment Studies, 'Metropolis: which perspectives? Cities, social life and sustainable development'*, Paris: Laboratoire de Psychologie Environnementale, Université René Descartes – Paris V.

Driver, B. L., 1990. 'Recreation opportunity spectrum: basic concepts and use in land management planning'. In R. Graham and R. Lawerence (eds), *Towards Serving Visitors and Managing Our Resources*. Proceedings of the First Canada–US Workshop on Visitor Management in Parks and Protected Areas. Waterloo, ON: University of Waterloo and Environment Canada, Parks.

Forman, R. T. T., 1996. *Land Mosaics*. New York: Cambridge University Press.

Francis, M., 1987. 'Some different meanings attached to a city park and community gardens. *Landscape Journal* 6(2), 197, 101–12.

Godbey, G., Graefe, A., and James, S. W., 1992. *The Benefits of Local Recreation and Park Services: a nationwide study of the perceptions of the American public*. Leisure Studies Program, Pennsylvania State University for the National Recreation and Park Association.

Grandison, K. I., 1999. 'Challenging formalism: the implications of contemporary cultural theory for historic preservation', *Landscape Journal* 18(1), 30–40.

Hall, P., 1998. *Sociable Cities: the legacy of Ebenezer Howard*. Chichester: Wiley.

Halseth, G., and Doddridge, J., 2000. 'Children's cognitive mapping: a potential tool for neighbourhood planning'. *Environment and Planning B: Planning and Design*, 27, 565–82.

Hart, R., 1979. *Children's Experience of Place*. New York: Irvington Publishers.

Haynes, J., 1983. 'Historic landscape conservation', *Papers in Local and Rural Planning No. 20*, Cheltenham: Gloucestershire College of Arts and Technology.

Hawkes, J., 1951. *A Land*. London: Cresset Press.

Hillman, M., Adams, J. and Whitelegg, J., 1990. *One False Move … A Study of Children's Independent Mobility*. London: Policy Studies Institute.

House of Commons Environment, Transport and Regional Affairs Select Committee, 1999. *Environment, Transport and Regional Affairs – Twentieth Report: town and country parks*. www.publications.parliament (October 1999).

Inland Waterways Amenity Advisory Council, 2001. *The Inland Waterways: towards greater social inclusion*. Final report of the working group on social inclusion. Rickmansworth, Hertfordshire: IWAAC.

Kaplan, R., and Kaplan, S., 1989. *Experience of Nature: a psychological perspective*. New York: Cambridge University Press.

Kaplan, R., Kaplan, S., and Ryan, R. L., 1998. *With People in Mind: design and management of everyday nature*. Washington, DC: Island Press.

Kelly, G. A., 1955. *The Psychology of Personal Constructs*. New York: W. W. Norton.

Macdonald, M., (ed.), 1992. 'Patrick Geddes; ecologist, educator, visual thinker'. *Edinburgh Review* 88, Summer 1992.

Mackay, D., 1995. *Scotland's Rural Land Use: the history and effectiveness in Scotland of the Forestry Commission, Nature Conservancy Council and Countryside Commission*. Aberdeen: Scottish Cultural Press.

McVean, D. N., and Lockie, J., 1969. *Ecology and Land Use in Upland Scotland*. Edinburgh: Edinburgh University Press.

OPENspace Research Centre, 2003. *Diversity Review: options for implementation*. Report for Countryside Agency. Edinburgh: Edinburgh College of Art and Heriot-Watt University.

Rivlin, L., 2000. 'The nature of found spaces'. In G. Moser, E. Pol, Y. Bernard, M. Bonnes, J.-A. Corraliza and V. Giuliani (eds), *Proceedings of the 16th Conference of the International Association of People-Environment Studies, 'Metropolis: which perspectives? Cities, social life and sustainable development'*, Paris: Laboratoire de Psychologie Environnementale, Université René Descartes – Paris V.

Rogers, R., et al, Urban Task Force, 1999. *Towards an Urban Renaissance: final report of the Urban Task Force chaired by Lord Rogers of Riverside*. London: Department of the Environment, Transport and the Regions.

Schuyler, D., 1986. *The New Urban Landscape: the redefinition of city form in nineteenth-century America*. Baltimore: Johns Hopkins University Press.

Scott, M. J., 1998. *The Environmental Correlates of Creativity and Innovation in Industrial Research Laboratories*, PhD thesis: University of Liverpool.

Scott, M.J. and Canter, D.V., 1997. 'Picture or place? A multiple sorting study of landscape', *Journal of Environmental Psychology* 17, 263–81.

Scott Myers, M., and Ward Thompson, C., 2003. 'Local Perceptions of Strathdon: perceptions by the people in Strathdon of their community and landscape' in S. Bell (ed.), *Crossplan: integrated, participatory planning as a tool for rural development*. Edinburgh: Forestry Commission.

Titman, W., 1994. *Special Places; Special People: the hidden curriculum of school grounds*. Godalming, Surrey: Learning Through Landscapes/WWF UK.

Ulrich, R. S., Simons, R. F., Losito, B. D., Fiorito, E., Miles, M. A., and Zelson, M. 1991. 'Stress recovery during exposure to natural and urban environments', *Journal of Environmental Psychology* 11: 201–30.

United Nations, 1993. *Agenda 21. UN Conference on Environment and Development, Rio de Janeiro, Brazil, 3–14 June 1992*. New York: United Nations Department of Public Information.

Ward Thompson, C, 1995. 'School playground design: a projective approach with school pupils and staff', *Landscape Research* 20(3), 124–40.

Ward Thompson, C., 1998. 'Historic American parks and contemporary needs'. *Landscape Journal* 17(1), 1–25.

Ward Thompson, C., Aspinall, P., Bell, S., and Findlay, C., 2002. *Local Open Space and Inclusion: case studies of use and abuse of woodlands in Central Scotland*. Report for Forestry Commission. OPENspace research centre, Edinburgh College of Art and Heriot-Watt University.

Wherrett, J. R., 2001, 'Predicting preferences for scenic landscapes using computer simulations', in S. Sheppard and H. Harshaw (eds), *Forests and Landscapes: linking ecology, sustainability and aesthetics*. Wallingford, Oxon: CABI.

Worpole, K., 2000. 'Regaining an interior world'. *Landscape Design* 289, 20–2.

Chapter 6

The environmental agenda
A personal view

Merrick Denton-Thompson

By drawing on my life in the public sector, I want to explore the context within which the landscape profession operates through a series of topics, all of which are confined to the south-east of England.

From time to time we all benefit from a deliberate reconstruction of our landscapes through design, but the landscape designer has little to do with our everyday environment. The organic and incremental growth of many of our towns and cities has been a direct response to circumstances of need and resources; their strong character and human scale were rarely deliberate consequences of conscious design. As for the rural context to these settlements, the landscape of the countryside is a pure by-product of the way we have chosen to settle and manage the land. As with our towns it is not until mass production begins to have a real impact that we respond by cherishing what is left of the old. It is, of course, too easy to dismiss the anguish that is often generated by new development as a product of our natural instinct to resist change. Resisting change is more commonplace when lives and the physical environment are in turmoil at the same time. The loss and erosion of cultural landscapes destroys the physical evidence of human behaviour responding to the circumstances of the time. These losses have an impact on us today as the sense of stability is lost.

All too often deliberate and conscious design becomes forced and, for whatever reason, loses the sought-after human connection. Many of the most successful designs are those that remain least obvious, but by far the majority of our most cherished landscapes have never been designed. Students of landscape design have, in the past, been actively encouraged by our schools of landscape to make prominent and distinctive design statements. This approach invariably ignores the cultural context within which the design is being contemplated. If replicated by all designers the total demise of cultural landscapes is certain.

I will illustrate my point by recounting the essence of a debate that focused on the merits or otherwise of the settlement of Poundbury, on the outskirts of Dorchester. One of my planning colleagues came back from a visit saying, "Poundbury had a great deal of merit. It was fairly densely developed, in the interests of sustainability, and people wanted to live there." This comment produced a tirade of ridicule from another planner and an architect friend, both declaring it to be pastiche. The second planner hated the idea of Poundbury's success because such culturally based development would be too constraining to meet today's needs. The architect deplored the idea of having to work on buildings where his options and freedom would be confined. It could of course be argued that Poundbury is denying the evolution of cultural developments by dwelling on what is comfortable and not aspiring to meet new challenges by creating the cultural landscapes of tomorrow. Poundbury may well have emulated the variations, scale of spaces and building materials of villages and towns in the region, but in so doing it is articulating the original cultural response to their development. People want to live there because they can relate to the place.

Society cannot afford the risks associated with allowing the design professions an empty canvas upon which design statements can be made every time new development takes place. If this were to be allowed the result would fragment cultural integrity and lead to total chaos. To be afforded the luxury of creating new physical environments through design carries with it enormous responsibility.

So profound has been the influence of information technology and mobility on society that I must face up to the stark probability that my children may not value in their lifetime the things that I value today. Is it my imagination, or is there already a revolution taking place in front of our very eyes? The young have always sought out the young, but there is new urgency, a new imperative, to the gatherings. In 1998 an extensive semiotic research survey was undertaken for the Learning Through Landscapes Trust into the attitudinal responses among adolescents generated by the external spaces they inhabit. One of the main frustrations felt by so many young people was the lack of high-quality spaces for them to be with their friends. What caught the researchers off guard was the desperate cry for tranquillity, and in many ways these are conflicting aspirations. Market research undertaken by MORI tells us that local government is failing the needs of young people, and yet we continue to ignore their needs in open space design and management. Being in transit to adulthood, young people fail to be regarded as important clients.

Advances in communication and the luxury of unrestrained mobility have had a huge influence on the structure of communities. The sustainability of the current extent of physical mobility must be in question, and the answer will determine how long term the changes that have occurred to those structures are. The suburban kitchen is not normally a welcome place for the neighbour any more. We can rarely choose who we live next too, and our mobility has enabled us to restructure our connections with others, satisfying our diverse needs through a multitude of communities many of which are fragmented and dispersed.

Choice, then, is being exercised, and we must then ask ourselves whether freedom to choose is a luxury that we can afford in the long term. The key question is how we choose to lead our lives and how this affects the living landscape. We have been seduced by unlimited choice, and we are too weak to resist it. We know now that the lifestyles of most of us in the developed world cannot be enjoyed worldwide, but we are not prepared to give anything up. Clearly advances in technology will open up opportunities to overcome many of the issues that we perceive to be unsustainable, but we cannot rely on such advances happening in the future as an excuse to continue to lead unsustainable lifestyles.

There is a political apathy on behalf of the electorate on long-term environmental issues. The deep-seated and possibly irreversible changes to the environment cannot be denied by society, and its lack of political profile cannot be tolerated for much longer. Theory has never been a great generator of policy change, and the politician will hide behind his or her electorate, who will only be activated by a disaster before pressing for changes. One of the problems that disguise and shelter society from its behaviour is caused by the nature of changes to the environment. The most obvious are incremental changes over long periods of time and the cumulative effects of a multiplicity of small impacts. The massive loss of biodiversity is a good example of this, as it has gone largely unnoticed by the general public. Irreversible damage to the environment is seen to be tomorrow's problem and something for our children to worry about.

Housing dominates the planning debate

In the UK the planning process has been hijacked by the housing debate since the 1970s, although this is mainly focused in southern England. We seem incapable of understanding that much of the projected housing need is generated by the way we choose to lead our lives. There are some good news stories underlying the figures. People are living longer and we are promised that life expectancy will continue to rise. The downside is the fact that we are living longer alone – and not just in our old age. For example, more than 1.25 million of today's projected households' needs are created by those aged between 15 and 45 who will not form a stable enough relationship to share a dwelling. Never before has the percentage of projected households been dependent on so big a change in social living. Is anyone prepared to question whether or not all the current trends are what we want from society? Children leaving home earlier and earlier, or not at all, the elderly left on their own and the pursuit of self in isolation from family or social responsibilities are now the norm.

A comprehensive vision for the society we want to live in is urgently required. The planning profession appears to be running scared of accusations of social engineering, but without questioning the forces behind the housing numbers we are just 'predicting and providing' and just pretending to 'monitor and manage'. We can do a great deal to influence this issue, through raising awareness and education, and neither should we shy away from using fiscal reform to influence the way we lead our lives. Neither side in the housing debate is facing up to reality.

The environmental consequences of pursuing the numbers without question are obvious. The first is the huge under-occupation of our existing housing stock. This is not the place to rehearse the full implications of this issue, but they include the inevitable use of non-renewable resources to build additional housing unnecessarily, energy use to sustain low-occupation buildings and a poor use of available resources for property management.

The second question is where to build, and here we come up against one of the main dilemmas facing both housing- and employment-related development: it is cheaper to develop greenfield sites than it is to re-use previously developed land. The British government has set targets for 60 per cent of new development to be located on brownfield sites but has given no indication of how this is going to be achieved. Of course, for much of the South East of England such a target is not achievable, because not enough of such land is available to meet the housing needs. If housing numbers are driven by changes in social living rather than projected birth rates and rises in inward migration, then changes in planning policy are needed. If the primary influence is based on the way the existing population chooses to live, then the sustainable approach to development is to meet the needs close to the generators of need. Take this to its logical conclusion and we must question the validity of continuing to protect the greenbelt from development. If we add to this policies for making the best use of existing infrastructure, of schools, of transport, etc. and the urgent requirement to reduce the need to travel, then the argument for actually targeting greenbelt for development is almost irrefutable. In protecting the greenbelt we are, of course, conserving space as a tool for defining our towns and cities. These areas are being protected for where they are rather than because of their important cultural, biological or visual characteristics, for which there is a well-tried and tested landscape designation mechanism in place, such as Areas of Outstanding Natural Beauty.

The public, however, have a right to expect planning policy to enhance and not destroy the strong sense of local identity. Coalescence of urban settlements can erode the sense of place and belonging, securing further decline in residual community strength. Retaining strategic and local gaps between expanding towns is an important consideration. However, we must have a vision for such gaps: how are they going to be managed and used? These places are declining in strength of rural character because of the paraphernalia of suburbia: signs, lighting and fencing etc. through to the development of golf courses, sports fields and 'horseyculture'.

The urban fringe is too valuable to turn our backs on. This is the place for government to be targeting increasing access to the countryside, close to where people live. Too many of our urban fringes have become a no-man's land, neither productive farmland nor useable space supporting urban living. If we are serious about the health of the nation and we believe in the fundamental concept of lifelong learning, then a new approach to the management of the urban fringe is necessary.

Connections between town and country

The migration of people away from our town and city centres has been going on for years because of the failure of our urban places to meet their needs. Recently this trend has been reversed in places where both urban renewal and cultural development have taken place. To what extent the trend can be comprehensively reversed remains to be seen; some might say that the aspiration to live in the countryside is so deep seated in the British culture that it is an impossible challenge. The solution may be found, however, as the young want to live in our towns and cities. The question then is this: what do we need to do to ensure that such places remain attractive when young people's needs change? We need safe, tranquil urban environments of high quality to live and work in, alongside easily accessible cultural assets such as clubs, bars, art galleries and theatres.

Merrick Denton-Thompson

Young people

The first challenge is to devise an urban form and put in place the management to actually welcome young people to our towns and cities. All too often the exuberance of youth ends in conflict with the urban environment. The obvious place to start is to explore the quality and resources of the places society already provides for young people: schools. There are some 36,700 schools in the UK, 7,000 of which are secondary schools. They occupy some 40,000 hectares of land, and although there has been some tangible improvement in environmental quality over the last 15 years, the majority remain in a very run-down condition. Most are dominated by the results of municipal thinking at its worst, from the sterile asphalt and uncompromising spaces left over from Victorian school development to the exposed and bleak grass with chain-link fencing that dominated the mass production designs of the 1960s and 1970s. These are the places we design for children, and we must ask ourselves whether they instil a sense of pride and belonging in our young people.

These bleak environments are the places where young people meet each other. They are the places society provides for them to begin to develop a role for themselves in society. These are the places where young people are

6.1
Children in an
asphalt landscape

forced together, where they will make friends for life, where they will make enemies – and yet there is no professional supervision or help. The time they spend outside is not seen as essential to their development, and yet the reverse is true. Even today there is no policy on the provision of outside seating in the environment of our schools. If we get the ingredients right we now know that positive social interaction will result, the number of accidents will fall dramatically and bullying will all but disappear. But the advantages of fully integrating the external environment into the ethos of schools cannot be overstated when it comes to furthering the resources available to formal education.

The Learning Through Landscapes Trust, set up in the UK in 1990, has done a great deal to change government policy on the way such land is managed, but it remains an area of activity that needs to be taken more seriously by those involved in child development. By understanding the needs of young people and involving them directly in the process of change the Trust has stimulated improvements to the education estate all over the country. By giving training, support and authority to teachers, governors and parents, the Trust has also created the opportunity for people to take charge of providing for the needs of our children. The results have been dramatic, with the creation of rich, intimate places for children to learn, either through play and social interaction or through more formal use of the external environment for direct learning through the National Curriculum. The Trust has undertaken an extensive research project into the interaction between young people and the external environment, especially in secondary schools. Not only do young people aspire to places of high quality and tranquillity, as mentioned earlier, but they have a deep sense of despair and degradation as a response to the appalling external environment we provide for them.

One of the most significant problems is that we have structured the school around only a small part of the child's development needs: the injection of the formal curriculum. Can we really justify such huge resources given over to only a part of the child's needs? We hear all too often of schools re-structuring the day by removing social time, meaning that the problems and challenges of connecting with other young people has to occur outside the school gate. In the UK today the secondary school is too often an underused urban resource, and this can no longer be tolerated.

The school ought to be a place where young people would like to stay 24 hours a day, rather than a place they spend all their time trying to avoid. Look at the way we handle eating and socialising in secondary schools. Even today some schools force young people to eat outside in cold and bleak environments not designed in any way for such activities. The introduction of 24-hour cybercafés, fast food, music, and other facilities for young people would begin the slow process of changing young people's response to such places

6.2
Young child
eager to learn

and begin the task of creating vibrant and exciting environments to live and learn in. The landscape of such places should be of the highest quality, lifting the horizons of young people, providing stimulating places to learn and to be with each other.

So, any new national initiative to regenerate urban areas needs to start by targeting those places that connect to key elements of the community; but, as in schools, the programme will not just be a change to the physical fabric of the place. Changes in management and culture will need to go side by side with these programmes if we are to keep up with evolution.

Urban regeneration

Programmes of regeneration must celebrate the existence of those features, spaces or buildings that contribute to the local scene, setting the character of the area or having a longstanding influence upon the local community. Such a strategy respects cultural features and consolidates the role such icons have in contributing to the sense of place. The challenge is to do this in a way that sparks a chain reaction whereby private investment follows public investment.

In Hampshire an urban regeneration programme, targeted at older parts of towns and cities, has been operating since the mid-1980s. Here the programme adopted the approach of identifying the key features that already played a part in setting the character but needed investment to reinforce the influence. Long life of materials, appropriateness and high quality were the three main policies pursued in the design and construction of the projects that were identified for investment.

The programme specifically targeted boundaries of places for investment. These were places that institutional organisations and private people had failed to invest in, despite the impact that neglect had on large areas of the urban environment. The programme included:

- reinstatement of railings to Victorian parks that had been taken out during the war years and had been replaced with chain-link fences;
- high-quality entrance ways to churches;
- reconstruction of footways using traditional stone paving at the frontages of important old buildings that had previously been in a sea of tarmac;
- cleaning important features of the townscape such as churches and war memorials;
- restoration of Victorian parks that had become threatening places because the original planting had not been managed for 40 years or so;
- projects to support the local economy, where changing and improving the setting to small runs of local shops made the shopping experience more enjoyable and as a result made the shops more viable commercial enterprises.

There was political support to take risks, and on several occasions the programme invested in private land to stimulate property owners to act to restore important buildings. This ran the risk of the authority being accused of spending public money in a way that benefited the pockets of private people, but the over-riding public benefit accruing from the programme ensured that

6.3
Reconstruction of
footways using
traditional stone
paving to the
frontage of
St Peter's Church,
Portsmouth
(designer Simon
Cramp): before

the accusation never emerged. At Peel Road in Gosport, we invested in the restoration of boundary railings and footways along the frontages of terraced houses, and as a result all the householders invested in redecoration and restoration. The injection of public money secured a radical increase in property value at the same time as stimulating a chain reaction in private investment.

But our urban areas need a much more profound and extensive programme of action. Linking people, place and the economy is crucial to the

6.4
Frontage of
St Peter's Church:
after

success of any new national initiatives. One of the key problems is the inability of urban areas to change quickly in response to a rapidly evolving set of circumstances. Too many places in the UK are in a process of long-term decline, and the resulting negative influence on the overall area is not fully recognised until it is too late.

Good ideas that have been around a long time, such as providing above-shop accommodation, need to be more actively pursued. Conversion to

high-standard residential accommodation of those retail properties that can no longer survive in the current marketplace is an obvious target for public investment. However, linked with this point is the failure of some planning authorities to adequately review planning policies that influence urban capacity. Things have moved on, and employment and residential zoning are a thing of the past. Mixed use is crucial to sustainable lifestyles. Perhaps new development is needed in the suburbs to achieve higher densities, at the same time making the best use of existing infrastructure. Somehow we have to break the automatic assumption that high density means low quality; equally we have to accept that smaller households do not mean smaller houses.

6.5
Peel Road, Gosport

For as long as it remains both easy and cost effective to develop greenfield sites, then that is where development will take place, closing down more opportunities of making the best use of scarce financial resources to reinvigorate our declining urban landscapes.

A mobile society

The planning system in the UK has been remarkably successful in securing the continuing separation of town and country, but perhaps not so successful is the

6.6
Road construction
destroys
irreplaceable
landscapes as seen
on Twyford Down

quality of the average development. It is, however, too late to prevent the tide of out-of-town shopping facilities that have grown enormously in the last 20 years or so. We are partly persuaded by the retail argument that propounds the advantages of one-stop shop policy, in the interests of reducing the number of journeys that are the cause of so much congestion in southern England.

Mobility is another theme that needs to dominate our agendas: how can we retain the same quality of life at the same time as reducing the need to travel? The commercial sector is, of course, very quick to count the cost of congestion to the economy in the move to obtain more investment in road construction. However, what is never counted is the cost of the loss of productive time to commerce that is inevitable when the car is chosen as the only method of moving around. Road construction has been a great destroyer of fine, irreplaceable landscapes, driven for so many years by a shallow system of justifying investment – the cost–benefit analysis (COBA) – where neither the direct short-term cost of environmental damage nor the long-term costs associated with promoting an unsustainable form of travel could ever be adequately assessed.

We cannot ignore the huge freedom that the car has brought, nor can we ignore the perception of safety that the car generates among women. It is so much part of our home economy and our way of life that it is perhaps unrealistic to assume that things can be very different. Advances in technology in the

6.7
Field of oil
seed rape

design of new engines must concentrate, as a matter of critical urgency, on renewable energy as a power source and on preventing the release of harmful gases into the atmosphere. We need to pursue new ideas. For example, in my own county 12,000 hectares of oil seed rape is grown each year, only half of which would be sufficient to be turned into biodiesel to power all the current bus journeys in the county for a year.

A realistic initial approach must be to make the best use of our existing road space, though again this would require some flexibility in lifestyles. We can take this view with some confidence, as it is quite possible to move around freely, without hold ups, in almost all parts of the country outside peak periods. The evidence is there – for example, in the obvious difference in road use between term time and the school holidays. Up and down the country there are various initiatives to encourage children to make use of other forms of transport, such as walking, cycling and the bus, but more needs to be done – we might even see the return of coat racks in schools! Information technology, flexible working patterns and multipurpose journeys could have a far greater impact now on road space use, but change in attitudes is slow to happen.

We waste too much

Lifestyle changes need the support of government and commerce. Taking the trip to the supermarket a stage further, we could ask why Sainsbury's cannot accept for recycling every item of waste generated from the shopping trolley? Intervention would be required to get retailers to comply, and they might begin to look very closely at packaging. At the same time, the buying public needs to look closely at its behaviour, which, after all, drives commerce to pursue particular policies in the first place. The problem is that local government is designed to shelter people from the consequences of their lifestyles, and it does this very successfully. If we speed when driving, local government erects traffic-calming paraphernalia; if we throw our 15-year-old out of the home, he or she will be picked up; we throw out our rubbish, but we rarely have to live next to the refuse tip. If lifestyle decisions are to be changed, we in local government must start the process of removing that shelter.

The waste we produce is another theme to the urgent changes we need to make in our lifestyle. Although we are recycling more every year, we are producing more waste each year, resulting in a net increase in waste production, which all too often must end up in a landfill site. In the UK this is a massive issue, because of the high ratio of population to land. Some European countries are much more advanced in dealing with this issue.

However effective we are in undertaking environmental impact assessments in site choice or in landscape restoration, we are just papering over the cracks of a fundamental problem. The science of waste burners, whether they recycle energy or not, is simply not trusted by the general public, but even this technology is planning for waste rather than moving society to a position where there is no waste. We must pursue the single path of sustainable lifestyles, where everything we consume is renewable and where consumption is 100 per cent efficient, and if there have to be residues they are planned for as assets for use elsewhere.

Long-term sustainability in everything we do remains an aspiration that our current political system is ill equipped to meet, because of the short duration of political timescales. The popular perception is that sustainability will result in our quality of life diminishing, and to pursue it will carry considerable political risk. The optimist would rightly point to the fabulous human ability to invent, but there is no greater challenge for modern-day society than attempting to live in a totally sustainable way and at the same time retaining the current quality of life as a result of advances in technology.

Multi-functional countryside

One of the greatest tactical flaws in the argument for sustainability occurred when the term first began to be used: the direct link with the word 'development'. To the person in the street development is all about change and invariably about the construction of something – houses, roads, etc. The perception today is that the main threat to the environment is through development, and yet the single biggest threat is caused by the way we choose to manage our natural resources. Nowhere is this more evident than in the way we choose to manage the country-side. The results of millions of day-to-day decisions about the way the country-side is managed, such as mechanisation and the use of chemicals, have largely gone unnoticed. This is despite the diffuse pollution of our water, devastating destruction of cultural landscapes (the historical environment), the huge loss of biological diversity and the erosion of the strong sense of place that has occurred as a result of those decisions over the last 50 years.

The English countryside is a by-product of the way we have chosen to settle and manage the landscape. The intervention system through the Common Agricultural Policy has one key objective concerning the production of food: traceable, safe and affordable food. That single objective, supported through subsidies, has largely been met, but the cost elsewhere is unacceptable. Society's agenda for the countryside has changed: we want much more than safe, affordable food. We want to conserve and improve the strong sense of place, we want a countryside rich in wildlife, and we want natural resources of soil and water to be conserved and improved. We also want improved access to meet today's lifestyles, for health and lifelong learning. We aspire to a multi-functional countryside secured through the integration of management objectives.

Across Europe the Common Agricultural Policy has taken some of the uncertainties out of farming through the subsidies given for production. Stability has been achieved, breathing life and investment into agriculture in the postwar years. However, this intervention has had effects that were not planned, particularly in the UK. The loss of mixed farms has arisen because farmers have not needed to spread the risk across the various sectors any more. Technological investment and mechanisation have removed the workforce from the land and changed the landscape to fit with machinery. Advances in chemical and biotechnological development in agriculture have removed wild-life from the countryside to such an extent that you can walk for miles in the countryside in midsummer and not see a butterfly. The reduced risk also prompted huge institutional investment in farmland, which pushed up the price of farmland to its current levels.

The historical environment has suffered huge losses and is still under pressure despite the obvious economic potential for tourism that conserving

6.8
Ploughed
round barrow, a
scheduled ancient
monument

and making it more accessible would have. Today we can still see the ploughing and destruction of scheduled ancient monuments funded by government subsidy at a time when we recognise that the value of agriculture is a tenth that of tourism. The contribution to GDP from agriculture is about £7.5 billion and that from tourism about £75 billion. However tourism has failed to re-invest adequately in its primary asset, 'the green and pleasant land', the foundation of the international image of this country. Farm bed-and-breakfast facilities will contribute to the rural economy, but they can only confer minor advantages to the management of the countryside, and a more extensive system of getting the tourist industry to invest back into the countryside is needed.

Over the years various attempts have been made to try to quantify environmental assets in financial terms, but as yet we have no method that stands up to scrutiny that can give values to such intangible characteristics as biodiversity, sense of place and attractiveness. Clearly the erosion of the historical environment will have an impact upon opportunities for tourism, and perhaps these impacts can be quantified in financial terms. We can also make the connection between current land management practice and the impact it has on diffuse pollution. The majority of key point sources of pollution of rivers and aquifers have now been identified and dealt with, with 80 per cent of all residual pollution now being of a diffuse nature. Diffuse pollution includes

particulates which end up blocking ditches and drainage systems and chemicals directly affecting water quality. For example, the water emerging from the
eastern end of the South Downs now has to be 'blended' to make it drinkable.
The estimated annual cost of dealing with diffuse pollution nationally is estimated to be in excess of £1.2 billion per year.

Nature conservation was re-packaged as a result of the World
Summit in Rio in 1992, with the signing of the Biodiversity Convention. The
system surrounding biodiversity action planning introduced a more systematic
and business-like approach to nature conservation. We have failed to convince
the person in the street of the need for urgency in conserving the planet's rich
biological heritage. This is reflected in the failure of society to recognise the
impact that modern farming systems have had upon habitats and species.
Today we can celebrate the scenic qualities of vast tracks of land designated as
Areas of Outstanding Natural Beauty that are at the same time completely
sterile, void of any wildlife interest. Yet the whole landscape experience is not
confined to the single sense of long views over rolling countryside, of the patchwork quilt, of trees, hedges and woods. The landscape experience is also about
micro-characteristics of sound, colour, taste, temperature and seasonal change.

John Gummer, when he was Secretary of State for the Environment,
announced the new obligations that we all had to protect biodiversity, and he
was right to identify both the moral and utilitarian obligations that we all have for

6.9
Chalk grassland
on Area of
Outstanding
Natural Beauty

conserving biodiversity. We in public life must go out of our way to reconnect society with the benefits of protecting and conserving biodiversity.

Hampshire is ecologically the richest county in the country, with 1,400 different native vascular plants and a vast array of associated wildlife. The utilitarian aspects referred to by John Gummer can be easily quantified when examining the "Hampshire weed", the yew tree. *Taxus baccata* contains 115 diturpines, which are naturally occurring chemical compounds. Two of these form the basis, through biological technology, of the drugs Taxol and Taxotere, which are used to treat ovarian and other cancers. What then of the other 100 or so diturpines? We have only scientifically described 13 per cent of this planet's plant and animal species, so the extent of our ignorance is awesome. We are handicapped by our failure to quantify the scale of missed opportunities resulting from the loss of biodiversity and that almost certainly will impact on the future of humanity.

The ongoing debate about genetically modified (GM) organisms is coloured by society's deep suspicion of the scientific world. People link recent disasters of bovine spongiform encephalopathy and foot and mouth disease to the failures of scientists, so it is hardly surprising that the enormous investment that some of the world's multinational companies have made in the world of biotechnology has such a poor image. So many of today's sustainability issues may well have technological answers, and it is inevitable that some of those answers will lie some time in the future with the modification of genetics. It is the power of the science that is so terrifying to the general public. It is the well-publicised cases, such as the insertion of genes from the Arctic goldfish into tomato plants to create an inbuilt protection against freezer damage, that sparks the public's imagination. It is the combination of that response with the loss of confidence in the privately funded scientist and the power of multinational companies that leads to the automatic objection to such initiatives as GM technology. The public is only too aware that GM may create a gateway to a new evolution, the consequences of which we cannot predict – an evolution created by human intervention that manipulates genetic material in a way that cannot happen through natural selection or everyday mutation; a powerful science that once released into the environment may never be recovered, where unknown effects would be irreversible. The well-publicised precautionary principle needs systematic definition, which will soon have to be an integral part of land management policies in Europe.

In the UK the 1995 Environment Act introduced the need for land management plans to be prepared by national park authorities. This act was followed by the Countryside and Rights of Way Act, which required local government to take responsibility for the preparation of land management plans covering Areas of Outstanding Natural Beauty. The latter act is an interesting piece of legislation that places a statutory obligation upon local government to

produce integrated land management plans that would direct activities with which local government has absolutely no involvement. If we value the landscape so much, then surely it must be right that we arrive at a national consensus on what we want from the countryside: a consensus that articulates clearly the need to integrate land management objectives. One way of achieving this is to extend the requirement of strategic land management plans

6.10
Recreation and access to the countryside in the Avon Valley

6.11
Seats: learning through landscapes

for protected landscapes to cover the rest of the country. We know from the experience of the last 50 years that government intervention has a profound impact on the very nature of the countryside, moulding and influencing it. If these interventions are to continue, then surely they must be linked directly to these wider aspirations that we have for the countryside. The decoupling of farm production from subsidy that resulted from the mid-term review of the Common Agricultural Policy has created a wonderful new opportunity for securing a more sustainable approach to the management of the countryside. Such decoupled payments will not stand the test of time unless public benefits from such investment are fully transparent.

The farming community rose to the new challenge facing post-war Europe. Now that society wants more from the countryside, farming is best placed to deliver the new agenda. It will have to accept that with or without intervention subsidies it must be accountable for its management decisions, because of the breadth and depth of the effects that those decisions have on the environment. The farming community feels isolated as a direct result of its own success, and only a small part of the voting public is now associated with agricultural practice. Reconnecting town with country is critical to the future of the land-based industries, and one of the ways of making that connection is raising the level of accountability.

6.12
Children learning
with countryside
ranger at
Westwood
Woodland Park,
Hampshire

Merrick Denton-Thompson

The landscape profession

Landscape professionals operating in the countryside must recognise that there is little room for an overt "design statement". We must play a strong but recessive role: strong in our pursuit of appropriateness, and recessive in promoting semi-natural outcomes. We must pursue all of our investment programmes by utilising local provenance at a time when we are just beginning to realise the devastating impact on invertebrates and the wider animal communities of unplanned genetic introductions. We must maximise the use of natural regeneration as an invaluable design tool in our drive for sustainable landscapes. The new map of England that maps distinctive character as it changes through a variety of influences is a great starting point for re-investing in the countryside. The map records the consequences of human activity, i.e. the cultural landscape, resulting in a rich diversity in landscape character, characteristics that can be defined and described, thus allowing for detractors from that character to be identified easily and dealt with. We can be at the forefront of re-investing in the countryside of Europe to meet the needs of future generations. The careful consideration of character and how it has been formed is as relevant to the re-investment in our urban environment as it is to the countryside.

We have, on reflection, been seduced by the riches (not necessarily financial) of development and change, rather than spreading our skills evenly across the management of existing resources which is the new imperative.

We need to help society articulate what it wants from a sustainable approach to urban regeneration, to new urban form and to a multi-functional countryside. We then need to pursue the principles of sustainability with a new vigour.

Part 4

The search for a creative way forward

Chapter 7

The future
Landscape design in the 21st century

Peter Neal and John Hopkins

In drawing together some of the key strands of the preceding chapters and in identifying key drivers that are increasingly shaping our landscapes, it is interesting to cast an eye back to the writing of Brenda Colvin. A founder member of the Landscape Institute in the United Kingdom, her *Land and Landscape*, first published in 1947, became one of the first standard books of the modern profession in Britain. Fundamental observations, outlined in the revised foreword to her book in 1973, still ring true many decades later:

> In our study of the artistry of our forebears – that is, in the history of landscape design, emerging as it did from the art of garden design – we find two opposite philosophical attitudes reflected in the humanised landscape of the world.
>
> At one extreme, the placid acceptance of things as they are, with humanity deferential to nature, as in Eden before the fall, gives rise to design whose objective is to follow and perhaps coax, rather than coerce nature. This we see expressed in the art, and especially the garden art, of the Far East. The opposite attitude of self-assurance and will-to-power is characteristically expressed in Latin countries by geometric and architectural treatment of land and plant forms.

Various gradations between the two occur and may often associate together happily enough.

The tendency of our age is towards ever greater domination of nature by man, though we are dimly aware that the last word will be with nature unless we can adapt our new powers to the crescendo of evolution without overriding the natural laws ensuring healthy survival and duration.[1]

These opposing 'philosophical attitudes' descend from the Greeks, and have characterised philosophical debate in the West since. Through the Enlightenment, this duality of thought was solidified by Descartes (ostensibly to prove the existence and therefore sidelining of God, which enabled scientific endeavour to continue without threat) and has driven our thinking, economy and political life ever since. Darwin, as Hopkins reflects in Chapter 2, provided the scientific rationale for a *competitive* socio-economic and political system based on these dualistic principles. This duality of thought also existed in the east of course (in China through Taoism and Confucianism), but they were viewed as complementary, mutually supportive tendencies within the *spectrum of existence*, not separate. Certainly, we are now much more than 'dimly aware' that nature will 'have the last word'. As we push at the very extremities of the planet's ability to sustain us, the profession of landscape architecture, with its core interests in human *and* natural process, is well placed to promote the necessary global paradigm shift from dualism to holism and bring the two philosophical attitudes together.

7.1
The grounds of Stourhead in Wiltshire, laid out by the banker Henry Hoare II in the 18th century, were described by Walpole as 'one of the most picturesque scenes in the world'. To this day, the view of the Palladian bridge and Pantheon is considered to be one of the most definitive representations of naturalistic English garden scenes in the country

The rich and elite of our forebears chose to import classical references from their Grand Tours to Europe. Now, our increasingly multicultural society, fuelled by cheap travel and information technology, has the ability to draw on an ever more eclectic mix of references. Indeed, the contributors to this book are a mix of well-travelled professionals who have and continue to live, work, teach and practise on most continents. As Denton-Thompson notes in Chapter 6, 'advances in communication and the luxury of unrestrained mobility have had a huge influence on the structure of communities'.

Also, as William Mitchell observes, 'when high-speed, digital telecommunications systems succeed the telegraph and the telephone, you get socially significant changes in everyday interactions'.[2] Today we have at our fingertips an ever widening geography of thought and practice on which to draw. At its extreme we are even beginning to master the ability to manipulate the very genetic material from which our landscapes are formed. Yet, as the boundaries of knowledge, technology and experience expand exponentially, we are becoming increasingly aware that our landscapes are intensely local, and that they impose real limits. In our post-industrial age in the west, the UK government's Urban Task Force noted that the 'ecological imperative' is one of the three most powerful drivers of change alongside the technical revolution and social transformation: 'The importance of achieving higher environmental standards in the places we build, as well as protecting existing natural environments from damage, is one of the greatest challenges of the next [21st] century.'[3]

Swaffield illuminates, in Chapter 1, the inherent dichotomies of landscape knowledge in his opening personal narrative on ways of 'knowing the world'. Reflecting philosophical tradition, he recognises that it is at once 'conventional and radical, universal and particular, global and local'. He quotes Nan Fairbrother's *New Lives, New Landscapes* in which she powerfully argues that 'new landscapes for our new lives must now be consciously achieved by positive and clear sighted adaptation of the habitat to our new industrial condition'.[4] This fundamentally 'modernist' conception of landscape must now be revised if landscape knowledge is to move, in Swaffield's terms, from 'the fringes of the intellectual, industrial and political centres of power' to the centre. Fairbrother's quote should be amended now to read 'our new post-industrial condition'. The irony is that, while we in the west now seek holistic solutions for post-industrial life and landscapes, nations with emerging economies – China in particular – are industrialising at frantic rates based on the old western model.

James Corner argued in *Recovering Landscape* that landscape has the potential to be a 'strategic instrument of cultural change'.[5] Swaffield agrees and challenges landscape professionals to use their landscape expertise and knowledge to move towards the centre ground of political debate, a challenge echoed by Hopkins. Swaffield is right: 'landscape can be a way to empower a wider range of participants in the planning and design arena … a polysemic way of knowing, expanding upon the diversity of landscape within culture and design, illustrating the richness and vitality of its continuing evolution'.

The following four sections of this final chapter – 'Working on the land: art', 'Working with the land: ecology', 'Working through the land: society' and 'Working for the land: sustainability' – identify further key drivers that emerge from the preceding chapters. They are intended to help empower landscape architects to become 'agents of cultural change' and to facilitate collaborative working to integrate political initiative with people and place so that together we can achieve holistic, cultured landscapes.

Working on the land: art

Within Colvin's spectrum of humanised, or cultured landscapes, it is easy to draw on many familiar places that represent the extreme 'will-to-power' over the land. For historical reference, one need only thumb the pages of the Jellicoes' *Landscape of Man* for copious examples of landscapes with a boundless 'attitude of self-assurance': the renaissance gardens of Villa d'Este and Villa Lante in Italy; Le Nôtre's work at Vaux-le-Vicomte, Chantilly and Versailles; and the Belvedere Palaces of Lukas von Hildebrandt in Vienna.

Jump a century or two and one is in the midst of what Kenneth Clark refers to as the 'Romantic Rebellion'. Romantic art was 'made shockingly natural – far removed from the tranquillity and sculptural forms of classicism'.[6] Clark's true romantics, including Goya, Blake, Constable and Turner, were at their zenith. It was a time when the masters of the English Landscape School – Kent, Brown and Repton – were in full swing; a time, as Tate records in Chapter 3, when 'the perfection of Landscape Gardening' consisted in 'the fullest attention to these principles, Utility, Proportion, and Unity *or harmony of parts to the whole*'. Yet throughout the 18th century, landscape art sought to represent an aesthetic of pictorial perfection – beauty ahead of utility. This impulsive and significant shift was, however, fundamental in changing understandings of the perception of place and the importance of the aesthetic of nature. Yet it was, again as Tate reminds us, Kent who made *the* most fundamental shift when he 'leapt the garden fence and saw that all nature was a garden'.

Fast-forward two further centuries, and these perceptions of place and the aesthetics of nature have been played out on a completely different stage. Whereas Kent, Brown and Repton developed their art on the private country estates of the wealthy, the emerging canvas for 20th-century practice was the public landscape of our towns, cities and countryside. The profession moved from satisfying the visions and ambitions of wealthy, landed individuals to fulfilling the mixed and complex demands of corporate boards, council committees and public agencies. Tate quotes the Jellicoes: 'it was only in the present [20th] century that the collective landscape has emerged as a social necessity'. Today, the majority of clients are multi-headed and increasingly have responsibilities to broader local, regional, national and, increasingly, global agendas. This can be and is, of course, positive. It does, however, require sophisticated, intelligent, well-informed leadership. As Schwartz notes in Chapter 4, the power of the practitioner is 'directly proportional to the desire your client has to have you involved', and, 'few public administrators, councillors or mayors have either the artistic ambition or knowledge about art, or artists, to know how to both direct and protect the artist while representing the needs of the community'.

In short, bold projects come from bold clients who combine leadership, vision, determination and business and political skills in equal measure. The Portland Open Space Sequence created by Lawrence Halprin and Associates in the mid-1960s for the Portland Development Commission is a good example. The commission was created by the citizens of Portland in 1958 and first chaired by Ira C. Keller, who was the main force behind the urban regeneration of their downtown. The commission initiated a number of 'grand projects', including the South Auditorium district. The entire scheme was both a planning masterpiece and an astute real estate enterprise, attracting middle-class residents back into the city centre and delivering more than $394 million in tax revenue by the time it was completed in 1974. Furthermore, it had at its heart one of the greatest set pieces of post-war urban landscape: Auditorium Forecourt. As Tate notes in his chapter, this project, in parallel with New York's Paley Park, is 'driven by strongly humanist intentions', providing 'abstractions of the essential materials of landscape architecture'. The forecourt incorporates 'both the ideas and the processes of nature, but not the actual shapes'.[7] For Halprin and lead designer Angela Danadjieva, a key objective was the exploration of the relationship of humans to nature through abstraction and art. Fittingly, the forecourt was renamed the Ira C. Keller Fountain in 1978.

There are two memorial designs that can be read as 20th-century transition points in the history of landscape design, one each from either side of the Atlantic. The first is Geoffrey Jellicoe's Memorial to John F. Kennedy at Runnymede, and the second is Maya Lin's Vietnam Veterans Memorial in Washington, DC (Plate 25). As Tate notes, the former was Jellicoe's self-asserted 'adventure into a new field, of Allegory ... the simplest of devices with which to captivate the mind'. However, the power of the design lies in the manipulation of human experience, the melding of emotion, object, knowledge and landscape. As Tate also notes, 'Jellicoe appears to have used his immense

historical knowledge to drive his design work'. Similarly, Maya Lin's memorial design melds emotion, object, knowledge and landscape: 'The monument may lack an American flag, but you're surrounded by America, by the Washington Monument and the Lincoln Memorial (on which the two wings of the memorial focus). I don't design pure objects like those. I work with the landscape, and I hope that the object and the land are equal players'.[8] What links these two projects is artistic vision responding to history, culture, *genius loci* and abstraction in an appeal to the universal, the monumental and the human: land and humans as equal partners.

Tate defines the over-arching purpose of landscape architecture as 'making places different', which, he asserts, is a *radical* exercise. Interestingly, this has resonance with the title of the 1996 monograph on Martha Schwartz, 'Transfiguration of the Commonplace'.[9] Tate asserts that such a radicalism is based on three fundamental values: firstly, understanding the *genius loci* (the 'bones and marrow', in Provost's words); secondly, 'leaping the fence' – artistic vision; and thirdly, understanding history. Tate recognises the role of Jellicoe's and Lin's landmark projects in helping to 'establish the conditions for the work of two of the most publicized current practitioners': Schwartz and Adriaan Geuze. Any contemporary exhibition of influential, international landscape architecture projects would include Tate's referenced projects: Schwartz's abstract landscapes at

7.2
The Ira C. Keller Fountain in Portland's Auditorium Forecourt Plaza. Designed by Lawrence Halprin with Angela Danadjieva in 1970 to represent the relationship of humans to nature, the intention was to interpret the ideas and the processes of nature and its mode of operations, rather than its results

Jacob Javits Plaza, the HUD Plaza, and the Mesa Performing Arts Center, all described in her chapter. It would also include Geuze's Schouwburgplein, Rotterdam, and his VSB Garden, Utrecht. Tschumi's 1980s' then-radical alternative postmodern manifesto for an urban park at La Villette (Plate 24), Caruncho's Mas de les Voltes, Spain, Andrew Cao's Glass Garden and Claude Cormier's Blue Stick Garden and Lipstick Forest would also be likely inclusions.

These projects certainly satisfy Tate's criterion for radicalism. However, although they are culturally important, it is not clear that they satisfy the need to link people, place, culture and natural process. They seem to reflect a limited view of the full potential of landscape architecture. John Dewey's philosophy, referred to in Hopkins' chapter, while arguing for the centrality of art in expressing the human–nature relationship, also argues for the role of artist as interpreter/facilitator – a theme that circumnavigates this book. Such a role for the landscape architect seeks to transcend both the need to move beyond art as a medium for self-expression, and subserviently meeting the needs of the client. Hopkins quotes Steinitz's definition of the artist as interpreter: 'the artist is one who seeks wisdom, understanding and knowledge and who displays that understanding with artistic skill'. If landscape architecture has the potential to be a 'strategic instrument of cultural change', then the challenge is to complement such wisdom, understanding and knowledge with our growing technical capabilities, in order to create landscapes that integrate human needs and natural process with artistic skill.

Working with the land: ecology

At the other end of Colvin's spectrum of humanised or cultured landscapes, we are developing greater scientific understanding and expertise in working with the land and its inherent rhythms. Concepts of landscape ecology (pioneered by Richard Forman and others) – patches, corridors and mosaics – now provide a common structure for working with the land as a living system. Such a structure also provides a valuable 'handle for land-use planning and landscape architecture, since spatial pattern strongly controls movements, flows and changes'.[10] Combined with the power of GIS, we are now able to build and manipulate huge quantities of data to build conceptual scientific models, analyse existing structures and visualise landscape change.

However, as Ward Thompson cautions in Chapter 5, we must ensure that the concepts of patches, corridors and mosaics apply to the human species also and to exploit the computer's potential in 'developing that ideal of participatory planning that Patrick Geddes promoted nearly a century ago'. It was Geddes, that near unique mix of planner and botanist, who conceptualised the triadic relationship at work in towns and cities of 'place, work and folk', and their geographical, historical and spiritual equivalents of 'synergy, sympathy and synthesis'.[11] These constructs continue to influence contemporary theories of sustainable urban land-use planning and design. Indeed, Denton-Thompson proves this by eloquently describing the context for both the 'moral and utilitarian obligations that we all have for conserving biodiversity' and the need to remove the opaque cloud that surrounds the mystery of biodiversity and the public understanding of it. However, he also cautions that society retains a 'deep suspicious of the scientific world', linking recent disasters in the UK of 'bovine spongiform encephalopathy and foot and mouth disease to the failures of scientists'. This popular mistrust of scientists is mirrored by a parallel mistrust of politicians *and* professionals. In the past, 'Trust me, I'm a doctor' may have worked; nowadays this is rarely the case. This is why it is important for scientists, politicians and professionals to engage with the communities they serve in order to build trust.

There is also the ever present danger that scientific expertise could eclipse our innate 'language of landscape'. Some would argue that our increasingly technically specialised and professionally focused lives, and consecutive generations of urban living, have stripped away our spiritual and intuitive understanding of landscape. Have we already lost our ability to interpret and shape the land in an innately harmonious manner that was second nature to past, vernacular generations? In her *Language of Landscape* (referenced by Swaffield) Anne Whiston Spirn argues that landscape knowledge preceded even formal language. Certainly the many accounts of indigenous people's everyday lives show how landscape knowledge is integrated through all the senses – 'embodied' rather than conceived or perceived – and also how landscape knowledge is expressed through their art.

Bruce Chatwin's *Songlines* conveys how completely differently Australian aboriginals 'embodied' and communicated their intimate understanding of their environment: 'In theory, at least, the whole of Australia could be read as a musical score. There was hardly a rock or creek in the country that could not or had not been sung. One should perhaps visualise the Songlines as a spaghetti of Iliads and Odysseys, writhing this way and that, in which every "episode" was readable in terms of geology.'[12] Similarly, Chief Seattl, a Native American Indian, wrote an eloquently concise treatise on the spiritual, embodied value of the land in a letter to the American president in the 1850s: 'Every part of this earth is sacred to my people. Every shining pine-needle, every sandy shore, every mist in the dark woods, every clearing, and humming insect is holy in the memory and experience of my people'.[13] Landscape, therefore, as Spirn suggests, is our native language where we find each culture, religion and community developing a distinct vocabulary of elements and patterns that can be widely, or narrowly, shared. Consequently, the differences and equalities of scientific and intuitive or 'embodied' knowledge need to be recognised.

7.3

The Federal German Garden Festivals, *Bundesgartenschau*, have been a regular focus for the exploration of landscape design and aesthetics. Pictured here is a naturalistic landscape from the International Berlin Festival held in 1985, illustrating the increasing shift away from horticultural display to the representation of native habitats and processes

It is clear, however, that through growing scientific expertise we are beginning to create more ecologically coherent and competent landscapes. Ecological planting was pioneered in northern Europe and reached a wider public though the likes of the German Bundesgartenschau Festivals during the 1980s and a burgeoning ecological parks movement. Today such practice is widespread, and one need only turn to the last chapter of Robert Holden's *New Landscape Design* to find a diverse range of projects, including Grant Associates' Earth Centre in Yorkshire and Murase Associates' Water Pollution Control Laboratory in Portland, Oregon.[14] Although Fairbrother's *New Lives, New Landscapes* was one of the first books to grasp the essential link between ecology and landscape design, we must move on from this broad vision of landscape as habitat adapted by humans for human use to one that is more holistic, less object led, more process led and fit for our new 'post-industrial' lives in the west. As Kendle and Forbes have succinctly summarised, 'While the early naturalistic styles primarily recognised a pattern, and the wild garden recognised a process, modern ecological approaches reflect both aspects. At its best the modern ecological approach is concerned with the recreation of functioning systems.'[15] It is through understanding process and pattern, and making them explicit in landscape designs, that ecology can underpin the work of landscape architects.

The challenge now, therefore, is to achieve our understanding of landscape intuitively, intellectually and scientifically. This is the challenge of Dewey as expressed by the Jellicoes: 'Can we also, as did the simpler past civilisations, turn scientific data into abstract thought and art, thus to sustain and identify ourselves as humans and not as animals in this extraordinary continuum?'[16] Change in approaches and attitudes may initially be driven by a deep-seated and innate ability that is culturally imprinted through successive generations on both individuals and communities. Swaffield recognises this in his own narrative: 'a hint of the science of landscape as process and pattern'.

Ward Thompson proposes an interesting way in which we can achieve this synthesis when she states, 'We need precise plans to define artistic visions, function-specific space, and the neat, safe and attractive parks that offer equity of access for all. But these plans may need to be within the "fuzzy" framework of an open space network that is dynamic in aesthetic and ecological status, allowing a larger mosaic, patchwork of changing, loose-fit landscapes.' These sorts of plans have been prepared for the 'hot spot' growth area of the Thames Gateway, in south-east England – a 60 km long regeneration corridor running either side of the River Thames from Tower Bridge to Southend on the northern bank and the Isle of Sheppey on the southern bank (Plate 27). The plans are promoted by the government's over-arching *Greening the Gateway* policy document, published in 2004.[17]

Thames Strategy East is one of a series of strategies being prepared at the sub-regional level along with the East London Green Grid, Kent Thames side Green Grid, the Thames Gateway South Essex Green Grid, and the Kent Medway regional park (Plate 28). These strategies provide the landscape, environmental and community context for radical change – up to 120,000 homes and associated infrastructure by 2016, much of it on post-industrial land. They are multi-functional spatial plans based on GIS data sets and supported by policies and guidance that address ecology, hydrology (including flood-risk management), archaeology and built heritage, climate change, planning, transport, the economy, urban form, open space, leisure, recreation, education and healthy living.

Working through the land: society

Ward Thompson also sets the scene for this section by attempting to answer the question of who benefits from landscape architecture. She highlights the complexities behind the obvious answer, 'everyone', and engages in a discourse that links with other contributors, including Swaffield, who says that 'recognising that what we know about landscape relates to why we need to know raises the fundamental question, whose way of knowing does it represent?' He continues,

'So much depends, however, on that modest word "we",' and quotes Bender: 'People's landscapes will operate on very different spatial scales … on very different temporal scales. … Each individual holds many landscapes in tension … landscapes are thus polysemic, and not so much artefact as in process of construction and reconstruction.' This is why public engagement is crucial, and why the appreciation of multiple processes is as important as product.

Denton-Thompson, as a county planning officer, is well placed to recognise that one of the problems 'is that local government is designed to shelter people from the consequences of their lifestyles' and that we must 'start the process of removing that shelter'. He also cautions that 'society cannot afford the risks associated with allowing the design professions an empty canvas upon which design statements can be made every time a new development takes place. If this were to be allowed the result would fragment cultural identity and lead to total chaos'. He goes on to express his despair at the failure of society to pick up the essence if not the detail of sustainability. His proposal that 'we must play a strong but recessive role: strong in our pursuit of appropriateness, and recessive in promoting semi-natural outcomes' has resonance with Ward Thompson's 'fuzzy frameworks' and 'loose-fit landscapes'. It also has resonance with the values, noted above, that Tate espouses: understanding the *genius loci*; 'leaping the fence' (artistic vision); and, finally, understanding history.

Ward Thompson quotes the European Landscape Convention, which 'sees the landscape as a key element of individual and social well-being as well as a component of cultural identity' that promotes 'landscape protection, management and planning and points clearly to the need for public and community consultation in developing landscape plans'. The convention is a huge step forward in recognising landscape as *the* issue for the future, addressing the interrelationships of people, place and process, social equity and environmental justice, and quality. She and Denton-Thompson raise the issue of rural communities and their development, management and protection. With 88 per cent of England designated countryside, but with only 20 per cent of the population living there and only 2 per cent directly engaged in agriculture or forestry, and with only 10 per cent managed for conservation, amenity or forestry, connections between our highly urbanised populace and the countryside are tenuous and fragile. Ward Thompson asks, 'What is the cultural vision for a rural landscape when cultivation – the root of all culture, both literally and metaphorically – is a receding prospect?' She concludes: 'There is a real challenge for landscape planning and community identity here'. Just as we are grappling with our 'post-industrial' landscapes, so we also need to grapple with our 'post-agroindustrial' landscapes.

However, with 80 per cent of the population living in urban areas, it has been recognised that the desperate condition of many of our urban areas must be addressed. The Urban Task Force report that was published in 1999 reinvigorated government policy and directed it towards sustainable development of higher-density mixed-use, mixed-tenure developments, based around public transport systems and high-quality environments predominantly on brownfield land. This was followed by the Urban Green Spaces Task Force, which published its report *Green Spaces, Better Places* in 2002.[18] It called for improved national policy for urban parks and green spaces. In response the government established CABE Space (part of the Commission for Architecture and the Built Environment – charged to promote higher quality in architecture and the built environment) as a champion for higher-quality parks, green spaces and the public realm through better planning, design, management and maintenance.

With regard specifically to urban parks, the cornerstone of our urban landscapes, Ward Thompson recalls Olmsted's vision that parks were for *all* people and then asks how much the designs of parks 'as opposed to their programmed use, need to change in the 21st century?' One answer can be found at Derby Arboretum, England, which was opened in 1848. Planned by J. C. Loudon, it is one of the first parks designed specifically for public use. Melanie Simo noted that 'the real beauty of the Derby Arboretum lay not simply in the eye of the beholder, but in the mind, and was dependent on an understanding of the site, the program, and the people of the town; and on the intellectual curiosity, scientific education, and awareness of the larger environment'.[19] A Conservation and Management Plan was prepared by LDA Design during 2000 in full consultation with the community and key stakeholders. The Heritage Lottery Fund awarded a £4.25 million grant in 2001, with matched funding from the City Council, and restoration and development were completed by 2005.[20] The objectives for the park, clearly documented by Loudon in 1845 and encapsulated in Simo's statement, were merely updated for the 21st century community, and drove the preparation of the management plan. The physical fabric – the design of the park – was changed very little, but was restored and renovated. However, new community facilities, such as the Heart of the Park building and a new wildlife area, were added, and a full programme of educational and recreational events and activities established.

While we are still grappling with models for the 21st-century park and improving our public realm, emphasis is increasingly being placed on management and long-term revenue funding. As an example, the government's 'cleaner, greener, safer' mantra emphasises 'liveability', or quality of life, in our urban areas. The Liveability Fund, some £89 million of public money, is intended to establish new ways of managing and investing in our urban public realm. Yet the question of funding for management of parks and the public realm have, at their root, a much more fundamental challenge: are communities prepared to tax themselves and pay for a high-quality public realm? The research evidence suggests that they are. The London Borough of Barking and Dagenham's MORI Budget Survey 2001 showed that 74 per cent of residents supported the priority of making the borough 'cleaner, greener and safer'; 60 per cent supported 'improving the general appearance' of the borough as a priority; 43 per cent said that the parks and open spaces were the most important priority for council expenditure – the second highest category after rubbish collection and street cleaning; 25 per cent said they would like to see an increase in expenditure to improve the service at the expense of other services (only 6 per cent supported less expenditure); and 57 per cent of residents said that parks and open spaces were the most used service that the council provided.

Evidence from the US confirms a similar message. The communities of Portland, Oregon approved a $135 million bond issue to purchase land and develop existing and new parks and open spaces – and they are not unique. Boulder, Colorado has had a dedicated sales tax to purchase land and to develop existing and new parks and open spaces since the 1960s. Business improvement districts have been established by communities in areas as diverse as New York City, Philadelphia and San Diego and are proving very successful in improving the quality of the public realm.

Communities, when presented with the facts in open and frank debate, are willing and able to make informed decisions about what is important to them: what they like, what they don't like, what they would like to see changed, and whether or not they are prepared to pay the consequent price to recoup the benefits, be they social, economic or environmental. Rebuilding trust between people, politicians and professionals by reinvigorating local democracy, and through consistent engagement, is crucial to achieving communities and communities of communities that can live sustainably.

Working for the land: sustainability

The argument for sustainable development has been won. The scale of the environmental impacts of our way of living in a finite world is now recognised. The 1987 Brundtland report set down the core principle of sustainable living as that which does not 'compromise the ability for future generations to meet their own needs'. Climate change is a well-recognised impact on the planet, owing to the release of greenhouse gases. Yet, despite Tony Blair agreeing that climate change poses the 'greatest challenge we face', and despite the Intergovernmental Panel on Climate Change concluding that 'most of the warming observed over the last 50 years is likely to have been due to increasing concentrations of greenhouse gases', the US remains implacably opposed to the actions promoted under the Kyoto Agreement, believing that they will negatively impact its economy. We desperately need more enlightened leadership from the world's remaining superpower, as the world's largest economy and polluter.

So although the argument for sustainable development may have been won, and delivering sustainable development has been recognised as a life-or-death challenge by most of the global community, we are not moving anywhere near fast enough. There are three things that must happen that integrate the themes discussed in this chapter with the three themes of sustainable development: the social, the economic and the environmental.

Firstly, social equity and justice must be the primary driver for local, regional, national and international development, and the destruction of our communities and our cultural resources must be reversed and minimised. This means reinvigorating democratic systems from the local to the global, and accounting for intergenerational – not just political – timescales. As Denton-Thompson notes, sustainability 'remains an aspiration that our current political system is ill equipped to meet, because of the short duration of political timescales' and because the 'popular perception is that sustainability will result in our quality of life diminishing'.

Secondly, local, regional and national economies and the global economy must be recast to take full account of and compensate for or offset any negative social and environmental impacts. This means that the success of any economy must be measured by quality of life indicators (as close a measure of happiness we can get), not gross domestic product and consumption.

Thirdly, the impact of our activities on the environment must be reduced to the absolute minimum: the use and depletion of natural resources; waste and pollution; the destruction of biodiversity and cultural resources. These should be the underlying principles uniting the planning, design and management of our landscapes.

The challenge is to live in a completely sustainable way while maintaining our essential quality of life. The following are offered as opportunities where landscape architects can make a contribution through their work.

Opportunity 1: restoring health to our post-industrial landscapes

Past industrial generations have polluted the land. However, we are now in a position to restore this land to full health for future generations. In the UK much development is now focused on previously used land: the government has set a target of 60 per cent of all new development occurring on brownfield land. Also, English Partnerships (the government's national regeneration agency) has an established coalfields programme addressing restoration of redundant sites, and it has recently established the Land Restoration Trust to promote viable and economic reuse and long-term management of previously used land. Innovative examples from Europe include Greenwich Millennium Village, England; Westergasfabriek, Holland; and Emscher Park and Völklinger Hütte (now a UNESCO world heritage site), Germany (Plate 26). Niall Kirkwood's *Manufactured Sites* describes these and other examples from the US and elsewhere.[21]

We now know that these restorations can be done in partnership with nature – for example, through the spontaneous revegetation of sites. Noel Kingsbury suggests 'there are two approaches to the use of post industrial vegetation. One is to manage what comes up by itself, so that the chaos of dereliction may be turned to ecological, functional and aesthetic advantage of a new landscape, the other is to learn from these natural test-beds in the creation of attractive but robust new plant mixtures for urban areas.'[22]

Opportunity 2: reuse, recycling and active stewardship of resources

Developing an approach to design that is resource neutral – with no net gain or loss of resources – poses a serious challenge. Current best practice aims for carbon-neutral or carbon-negative development as a measurable, achievable, overarching standard. One of the most significant examples in the UK is BedZED by the BioRegional Development Group and Peabody Trust, designed

7.4
Northala Fields, London, was designed by Art2Architecture in collaboration with Peter Neal and EDAW in 2003 as a synthesis of art, ecology and play. It is, in principle, a process-created landscape where every feature – including earth mounds, infrastructure, wetlands and grassland habitats – is formed primarily from recycled and reclaimed material

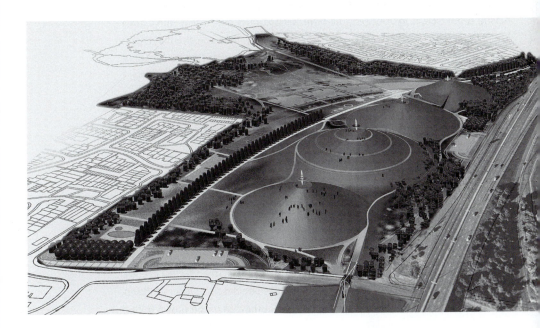

by Bill Dunster.[23] Some projects are looking to actively reuse material on site or imported onto the site, such as at Northala Fields, London. This requires a more organic and innovative design process that is undertaken in 'real time' during construction rather than ahead of construction, a process that is beginning to fuse design and construction activities.

In the UK, several masterplans are now in preparation that attempt to be self-sufficient in terms of water and energy. Landscape planning and design has a major role to play in managing fluvial and tidal flood risk; water collection, storing and cleansing; biofuel/mass production; and ameliorating climatic effects such as solar gain, heat-island effects, directing and channelling winds for cooling and air cleansing, and shelter from prevailing winds. These multifunctional landscapes also protect, enhance and create new, rich and diverse habitats that are good for humans and wildlife.

Opportunity 3: fusing management and maintenance with design and addressing funding in perpetuity

An increasing challenge is to factor in whole-life costings for projects, based on sustainable principles. Simply put, if you cannot afford to manage and maintain in perpetuity the resource you are creating, largely through the use of natural processes rather than capital resources, you shouldn't do it. Management is a recurring theme throughout this book. Tate notes that Schwartz 'compared having a landscape to "deciding to have a child or a pet: if you don't have enough money to build or care for the project properly, then you shouldn't have it",' and quotes Michael van Valkenburgh's observation that 'the way people execute landscapes is comparable to getting a dog, putting it in the basement and going to look how it's doing two years later'.

We need to establish whole-life costs for projects so that early in their inception one can establish sustainable funding streams for establishment and management in perpetuity. This should include their complete renewal at the end of their life cycle, which may be 25, 50 or 100 years, if necessary. This will force us to build more robustly. If a landscape is valued and has value, it will be protected and managed; if it is not valued or does not have value it won't be. We should be looking for all opportunities to ensure that the landscapes we create 'add value' and create ongoing economic benefits where possible. Of course, in the case of the town garden or square, these benefits might be purely for the 'public good' – this is for the community to decide. It must be recognised that the public park and the public realm generally are classic 'public goods' in economists' parlance, justified in being paid for purely out of the public purse.

However, in many instances there are opportunities to create 'working landscapes' that do create value and revenue.[24] We need new fiscal mechanisms to establish the economic returns of landscapes and find more creative ways to undertake cost–benefit analyses that include the ability to capture and return adjacent uplift in land values achieved through environmental improvements. Economic and revenue benefits of landscapes derive from multi-functional benefits such as flood-risk management, access and movement by foot and bicycle, air quality, biomass production, organic food production, leisure, tourism and recreation, as well as less tangible benefits such as physical and mental health benefits, social cohesion, biodiversity and nature conservation, and safety, security and perceptions of crime.[25] It is important that these values are increasingly factored into the economic appraisal of projects.

In her thoroughly researched book *Open to the Sky*, Malene Hauxner documents the second phase, in her view, of the modern breakthrough from 1950 to 1970 in 'building and landscape, spaces and works, and city landscapes'.[26] She asserts that through this period 'beauty lay in the man-made, the garden became the domain of the builder and the gardener; the aesthetic of the gardener prevailed over that of the manager'. It is clear now that 'the aesthetic of the gardener', as Hauxner puts it, must merge with that of the 'manager' and that still too much current garden, landscape and city design is about the former only. Denton-Thompson recognises this when he notes that 'we have, on reflection, been seduced by the riches (not necessarily financial) of development and change, rather than spreading our skills evenly across the management of existing resources'.

Armed with a greater understanding of *process*, we increasingly need to fuse planning, design, management and long-term maintenance. As examples, the new perennial plantings promoted by James Hitchmough and Nigel Dunnett of Sheffield University illustrate the move from static horticultural constructs to increasingly dynamic ecological structures.[27] Fundamental to this approach is the increasing aesthetic appreciation of the whole-life landscape, from stylised nature, through biotype planting to habitat restructuring. Christopher Lloyd's work at Great Dixter is a classic, but different, example of understanding the history of place and bending the serendipity of natural process to aesthetic effect. He provides an enlightened model for a future where the landscape manager is at least as important as the designer.

The cultured landscape

It is clear that our current generation, in the west at least, has to face new challenges brought on by the need to establish more sustainable forms of development. We need to respond to the transition from industrial and agri-industrial

7.5
The gardens of
the 15th-century
manor house of
Great Dixter in
East Sussex were
repaired and
enlarged by
Lutyens and
Jekyll in 1910.
Now home to
Christopher Lloyd,
the gardens are
increasingly seen
as a seamless
fusion of the
processes of
design, long-term
management and
skilled maintenance

societies to post-industrial and agri-industrial societies. This increasingly forces us to break new ground and develop new rationales and approaches to our work. Many of our urban and rural centres and landscapes, originally created to serve the demands of industry, commerce and food production, are in need of new purposes and identities capable of delivering an urban and rural renaissance.

We are becoming increasingly adept at restoring despoiled and polluted landscapes left as a legacy of our manufacturing past, and through this we are developing new aesthetic and cultural values for these landscapes. Alongside, there is an increasing desire to work with, rather than control, the natural processes and rhythms that have always shaped our environments.

Such changes can be mapped to a greater or lesser extent in many of our contemporary landscapes. But some, such as the work of Richard Haag in the US north-west during the 1970s and 1980s, really stand out. His Gas Works Park (1971–88), a 20-acre abandoned power generation site in Seattle, exploded the near universal view of what an urban park should look like. Here we began to reappraise the beauty and after-use of our industrial legacy. In parallel, the Bloedel Reserve Gardens (1979–84), within the 160-acre Bainbridge Island estate, sought a synthesis of human and natural worlds that drew on an intimate appreciation and respect for natural processes and structures. Elizabeth Meyer observed that the 'Gas Works and Bloedel reflect histories of both human actions modifying natural rhythms and natural events modifying human rhythms; both can be understood as disturbed'.[28] In a similar vein, Henri

Lefebvre suggests that 'the departure point for this history of space is not to be found in geographical descriptions of natural space, but rather in the study of those natural rhythms, and the modification of those rhythms and their inscription in space by means of human actions'.[29]

It is interesting to now see how Brenda Colvin's once opposing aesthetics from the eastern and 'Latin' cultures are beginning to unite. One could suggest that this is most evident at the very geographical boundaries where the two cultures meet. Take, for example, recent work in Sydney and California by George Hargreaves. His collaborative Millennium Parklands at Sydney's Homebush Bay provides a self-sustaining environmental framework for both the 2000 Olympic Games and the development of Newington, a 90-hectare new community that started life as the Olympic Village. The parklands have been created from what was originally a highly caustic mix of salt plant, brickworks, chemical facility and munitions depot. Through intensive bioremediation, the parklands fuse a distinct design aesthetic with a self-sustaining and fully functional network of freshwater and estuarine wetlands, tidal creeks, woodlands and grasslands.

Hargreaves extended this philosophy in San Francisco's newest park at Crissy Field, once home to the US 6th Army's military installation at the Presidio. Ahead of the restoration and rehabilitation of a native wetland and dune ecosystem, around 87,000 tonnes of hazardous material and a significant

7.6
The Millennium Parklands at Homebush Bay were one of the greatest legacies of Sydney's Olympic Games, held in 2000. Designed by Hargreaves Associates and EDAW, the 450 hectare site is now Australia's largest metropolitan park and includes fully functioning river networks, tidal estuary systems, saltmarsh communities and grasslands

amount of contaminated land required treatment. The project integrates a popular and diverse set of recreational facilities for a busy city, with a vigorous and dynamic environment, while still retaining many enduring historical and cultural references of the original Presidio complex. Described by Hargreaves as a 'human-made natural resource', Crissy Field is fundamentally about putting a system in place rather than creating a set piece. Here, natural processes are very evident, overt and legible.

This increasing trend for landscapes to be driven by natural processes has created a growing number of schemes that are as much system led as design led. Recent international competitions for both Downsview Park in Toronto and Fresh Kills in New York provide a clear illustration. The 1999 competition for Downsview, formerly a 320-acre military air base, encouraged submissions from a wide technical base, including ecology, graphics and landscape. Seen by the Canadian Government as its first national *urban* park, it was proposed as the antithesis of the country's existing system of national *wilderness* parks. A goal was to revitalise urban ecological systems that were to be as much social as natural. Tree CITY, a multidisciplinary collaboration between Rem Koolhaas, Bruce Mau Design and Arup among others, became the jurors' final selection, with its mix of randomness and choice that characterise current living conditions. 'It proposes a kind of hybrid state of park lands, tightly

7.7
Crissy Field, part of San Francisco Bay's waterfront and previously home to a US 6th Army base. Hargreaves Associates completed the initial phase of restoration in 2000, choosing to re-establish a fully functioning tidal salt marsh in part of the 40 hectare scheme in which natural processes are to be clearly evident, palpable and readable

connected to the urban surroundings, yet clearly autonomous as a site of trans-formed nature where many individual and communal desires can be indulged.'[30]

 The proposals for Fresh Kills on the western shore of Staten Island seek to facilitate semi-autonomous urban ecological systems to rebuild despoiled land. Sponsored by New York's Mayor Giuliani in 2001, and centred on the restoration of the Fresh Kills landfill, it is predominantly about remaking a new urban landscape from some of the most hostile and obnoxious constitu-ents – 150 million tonnes of human waste and rubbish. Field Operations, the selected practice led by James Corner, was supported by a team that included Arup, Applied Ecological Services, and Tomato. The proposals seek to reconsti-tute a matrix of diverse life forms and evolving ecologies described as *Lifescapes*. Fundamental to the proposals is the complete reversal of the site's identity and purpose – from putrid unsustainable landfill of unsavoury reputa-tion, to an expansive 'nature sprawl' providing a network of greenways, recre-ational open spaces and restored habitat reserves. It is planned that Fresh Kills Reserve will become 'a new nature-lifestyle island, both destination and envy of the surrounding urbanites'.[31] This offers an important construct for many other despoiled post-industrial urban environments. It recognises that the site's existing biodiversity is far richer than many comparable rural landscapes. Through a diverse mix of restored and new habitats, it will make a fundamental contribution to the health of larger ecosystems, including estuarine environ-ments, nesting sites and migratory routes. Critically, the project marks a stra-tegic repositioning of Staten Island's identity to a highly desirable place to live and raise children, and relies to a significant part on facilitating the creation of semi-independent ecological systems to achieve this aim.

 In Britain, we have potent opportunities to draw both on the emerging concepts being developed for Downsview and Fresh Kills and on established practice from the Millennium Parklands and Crissy Field. In the areas of housing growth identified in the government's *Sustainable Commu-nities Plan*, initiatives such as 'Greening the Gateway' for the Thames Gateway and its supplementary strategies, referred to above, will establish integrated networks of multi-functional green, or environmental, infrastructure, as it is increasingly being called. Elsewhere, the Nene Valley Regional Park and the Luton and Bedfordshire Green Infrastructure plans will similarly create new landscapes for urban, suburban and rural communities. Landscape is also emerging as a new driver of identity and character, re-establishing the attrac-tiveness and competitive advantage for the government's Housing Market Renewal Areas in the industrial Midlands and North of England. These initiatives should establish fully functioning 'lifescapes' on a scale never achieved before.

The Victorians had little doubt about the economic and social value of good-quality landscapes. This is particularly evident in their wonderful legacy of urban parks. We need to rebuild this consensus and articulate clear environmental values and benefits. Perhaps one of the greatest opportunities for our generation is to take the individual urban, suburban and rural landscape legacies and fragments and join them together in a vast 'working landscape' that meets social, economic and environmental imperatives. In doing so we would create our own legacy of connected, fully functioning environmental systems on a scale that has never been seen before. As evidenced by the examples described in this chapter, we have the technical ability, if the political and community will is there. In the 1970s, Ian McHarg encouraged us to 'design with nature', and through GIS, ecological theory and innovative technical ability we are now much better placed to work with the inherent processes and energies that abound in nature so as to enrich the lives of both current and future generations.[32] But to do this we must surrender some of our control in the process and put in place mechanisms to nurture the very best that humans working together with nature can achieve. For then, and only then, will we be able to create truly *cultured landscapes* hinted at by Colvin, where 'the placid acceptance of things as they are, with humanity deferential to nature, as in Eden before the fall, gives rise to design whose objective is to follow and perhaps coax, rather than coerce nature'.

Notes

1 Colvin, Brenda; Foreword, *Land and Landscape*; London: John Murray; 1947 (rev. 1973).

2 William Mitchell; *E-Topia: 'Urban life Jim – but not as we know it'*; Cambridge, MA: MIT Press; 1999.

3 Urban Task Force; *Towards an Urban Renaissance*; London: E. & F. N. Spon; 1999.

4 Fairbrother, Nan; *New Lives, New Landscapes*; London: Architectural Press; 1970.

5 Corner, James, ed.; *Recovering Landscape: Essays in Contemporary Landscape*; New York: Princeton Architectural Press; 1999.

6 Clark, Kenneth; *The Romantic Rebellion*; London: John Murray; 1973.

7 Halprin, Lawrence; *Process Architecture No. 4*; Tokyo: Process Architecture Publishing; 1978.

8 Hess, Elizabeth; 'A Tale of Two Memorials'; *Art in America*; April 1983; pp. 120–7.

9 Landecker, Heidi (ed.); *Martha Schwartz: Transfiguration of the Commonplace*; Washington, DC: Spacemaker Press; 1996.

10 Forman, R., Dramstad, W. and Olson, J.; *Landscape Ecology Principles in Landscape Architecture and Land Use Planning*; Washington, DC: Island Press; 1996.

11 Welter V; *Biopolis: Patrick Geddes and the City of Life*; Cambridge, MA: MIT Press; 2002.

12 Chatwin, Bruce; *The Songlines*; London: Picador; 1988; p.16.

13 Chief Seattl; *No Quiet Place*, Hastings: Hastings Arts Pocket Press; 1854.

14 Holden, Robert; *New Landscape Design*; London: Laurence King; 2003.

15 Kendle, T. and Forbes, S.; *Urban Nature Conservation*; London: E&FN Spon; 1997.

16 Jellicoe, Geoffrey and Susan; *The Landscape of Man: shaping the environment from prehistory to the present day*; London: Thames & Hudson; 1975 (rev. 1987); p. 391.

17 Office of the Deputy Prime Minister; *Greening the Gateway*; London: ODPM; 2004.

18 Office of the Deputy Prime Minister; Urban Green Spaces Taskforce; *Living Places: Cleaner, Greener, Safer*; London: ODPM; 2002.

19 Simo, Melanie; *Loudon and the Landscape: From Country Seat to Metropolis, 1783–1843*; New Haven: Yale University Press; 1989.

20 Derby Arboretum Conservation and Management Plan; London: LDA Design; 2000.

21 Kirkwood, Niall (ed.); *Manufactured Sites: Rethinking the Post-Industrial Landscape*; London: Spon Press; 2001.

22 Kingsbury, Noel, in Dunnett and Hitchmough (eds); *The Dynamic Landscape*; London and New York: Spon Press; 2004; p.73.

23 See www.bioregional.com

24 CABE Space; *The Value of Public Space: How High Quality Parks and Public Spaces Create Economic, Social and Environmental Value*; London: CABE Space; 2003.

25 LDA Design; South Essex Green Grid; Thames Gateway South Essex Partnership; 2005.

26 Hauxner, Malene; *Open to the Sky*; Copenhagen: Danish Architectural Press; 2003.

27 N. Dunnett and J. Hitchmough (eds); *The Dynamic Landscape: Design and Ecology of Landscape Vegetation*; London and New York: Spon Press; 2004.

28 Elizabeth Meyer, in William Saunders (ed.); *Richard Haag, Bloedel Reserve and Gas Works Park*; New York: Princeton Architectural Press; 1998.

29 Henri Lefebvre (trans. Donald Nicholson); *The Production of Space*; Cambridge, MA: Basil Blackwell; 1991.

30 Julia Czerniak (ed.); *Downsview Park Toronto*; New York: Prestel Verlag; 2001.

31 Field Operations; *Lifescape, Fresh Kills Reserve, Staten Island, New York*; www.nyc.gov (accessed 14 July 2004).

32 McHarg, Ian; *Design with Nature*; Chichester: John Wiley & Sons; reprinted edition, 1995.

Index

Page numbers in *italics* refer to illustrations

Index